I0832170

IMAM ALI

THE NOBLE HEART OF HUMANITY

A Life of Courage, Compassion, and Truth

DR. ABRAHAMKHOUREIS, PH.D.
NARRATOR OF AUTHENTIC HISTORY

Copyright Notice

Copyright © 2026 by ANG Power Publishing House.
All Rights Reserved.

No part of this publication, including but not limited to IMAM ALI: The Nobe Heart of Humanity, may be reproduced, stored in a database or retrieval system, or distributed, or transmitted in any form or by any means, including photocopying, recording, or other electronic or mechanical methods, without the prior written permission of the copyright holder, except in the case of brief quotations embodied in critical reviews and certain other noncommercial uses permitted by copyright law. For permission requests, write to the copyright holder at the address below.

ANG POWER PUBLISHING HOUSE
PO BOX 10735 / Glendale, CA 91209-USA
ANGPowerPHouse@Gmail.com
ISBN: 978-1-966837-55-8

This publication contains proprietary information pertaining to IMAM ALI: The Nobe Heart of Humanity. Unauthorized use, duplication, or adaptation of the concepts, graphics, or other materials within is prohibited and punishable under applicable laws.

Disclaimer: The author and publisher have made every effort to ensure the accuracy of the information in this publication. However, they assume no responsibility for errors or omissions or for any consequences resulting from the use of the information provided. This book is intended for educational and informational purposes only and does not constitute educational, professional or legal advice.

All trademarks, service marks, product names, and logos referenced in this book are the property of their respective owners. The contents of IMAM ALI: The Nobe Heart of Humanity is the intellectual property of Dr. Abraham Khoureis and is protected under copyright law.

Printed in the United States of America

Disclaimer

This book is a work of literature inspired by true events. While it draws from historical accounts, traditions, and collective memory, certain characters, dialogues, and scenes have been adapted for narrative purposes. Although it is based on accurate historical resources, it is not intended to serve as a definitive historical record.

Any resemblance to actual persons, living or deceased, as well as to organizations, institutions, governments, or groups, beyond the well-known historical figures and entities referenced, is entirely coincidental and unintentional.

The purpose of this work is to honor the essence of events and to explore their moral, spiritual, and human significance through the medium of authentic and real storytelling.

Table of Contents

Where Humanity Begins

"People are either your brother in faith, or your equal in humanity." Imam Ali

That single line carries a weight that entire institutions struggle to teach across years of study. It does not divide, it does not elevate one above another, and it does not allow the mind to escape into preference or prejudice. It anchors the human being in a simple truth, one that demands consistency in how we see, judge, and treat others. This is not philosophy for discussion alone; it is a standard for living.

To say that every educational institution, every university, every place of higher learning ought to have a department dedicated to Imam Ali's name and teachings is not an exaggeration. It is, in many ways, a correction. Because what is education if it sharpens the mind but leaves the moral center unattended. What is knowledge if it produces brilliance without balance, intelligence without restraint, power without justice.

His teachings offer something many modern systems have failed to preserve. They connect intellect with accountability. They remind the learner that knowledge is not an achievement in itself, it is a responsibility. When he spoke of justice, he did not speak of it as an abstract virtue, but as a lived obligation. When he governed, he did not separate leadership from humility. When he judged, he did not allow personal interest to cloud fairness. These are not lessons confined to history, they are frameworks for today.

Imagine a department built not merely to study his words, but to live them, to test them, to apply them across disciplines. Law students examining justice not only through statutes, but through moral clarity. Business students learning that profit without ethics is failure in disguise. Medical students reminded that care begins with seeing the patient not as a case, but as a human being equal in dignity. Political science students confronting the idea that leadership is not dominance, but service under scrutiny of one's own conscience.

Such a department would not belong to one religion, nor to one culture. It would belong to humanity. Because the statement itself refuses limitation. It does not say people are equal only if they believe as you do. It does not grant dignity conditionally. It establishes a universal ground where every human being stands, either as a brother in faith or as an equal in humanity, and in both cases deserving of justice, respect, and compassion.

What makes this vision necessary today is not only the beauty of the teaching, but the absence of it in practice. We live in a time where education has advanced in technology, in research, in specialization, but struggles with division, intolerance, and ethical compromise. We have produced experts who can solve complex problems, and sometimes fail at the simplest human responsibility, to treat another with fairness and dignity.

This is why such a department would not be ornamental. It would be essential. It would serve as a reminder within institutions that knowledge without moral direction is incomplete. It would challenge students and leaders alike to examine not only what they know, but how they act, not only what they achieve, but who they become in the process.

And perhaps more importantly, it would restore something that has been quietly neglected. The idea that education is not only about preparing individuals for careers, but about preparing them for humanity itself.

If there is one figure whose life and words deserve such a place, it is Imam Ali. His reverence matters, also, his relevance.

"People are either your brother in faith,
or your equal in humanity."

If the above sentence were truly understood, deeply taught, and consistently lived, entire systems would begin to change. Not by force, nor policy, but by the subtle transformation of those who pass through them.

Preface

There are moments in a writer's life when a truth enters quietly, almost without announcement, and begins to reshape how he sees the world. For me, that moment arrived as I spent years studying leadership, compassion, human struggle, and the timeless qualities that make souls rise above their circumstances. I had written about leaders in organizations, leaders in nations, leaders in families, leaders who rise and leaders who fall. But I had not fully understood what pure, uncompromised, human leadership looked like until I returned to the writings and the story of one man.

Imam Ali.

The term *Imam* in Arabic means a religious leader, a guide, or a teacher. It is a word that carries both spiritual and moral weight. In relation to this extraordinary man, and out of deep respect for his life and character, I will refer to him throughout this book as **Imam Ali** rather than simply Ali. At times, the traditional salutation of respect may also follow his name, as is customary among those who hold him in reverence. This is not meant to create distance between the reader and the man, but to honor the dignity, character, and example he left behind.

I did not discover him through a single book or a single miracle. I discovered him the way a person discovers a mountain: first from a distance, then by climbing closer, and finally by realizing that its height is greater than what the eyes first measured. Through history, sermons, letters, and stories preserved by generations, I began to understand his greatness. Through my family, and the values passed quietly from fathers to sons and mothers to daughters, I recognized his presence long before I knew his biography. And through his words, spoken more than fourteen centuries ago, I met a man whose clarity still speaks to the world today.

He was the chosen son-in-law of the last Messenger of God. That alone speaks to his character because great men choose companions of great integrity. He married a woman whose purity is recognized across the Muslim world, Lady Fatima, the daughter of the Prophet. If Christianity honors Mary as the symbol of devotion and purity, then Islam honors Fatima in a similar light: a holy daughter, a devoted wife, and a mother purified by God whose presence shaped history.

To understand Imam Ali, you must understand the home from which he grew. A home built on mercy. A home built on trust and compassion. A home that carried revelation, truth, and responsibility. Through that home, Imam Ali was not only a companion in the Prophet's mission; he became its guardian after the Prophet's passing, the conscience that refused corruption, the leader who placed unity above his own lawful right, the man who lived truth even when truth cost him everything.

As a student of leadership, I approached the story of Imam Ali expecting to find courage, intelligence, and strength. I found them. But beyond them, I found something deeper: a humanity so sincere and so unprotected that it made greatness accessible. Imam Ali's greatness does not come from distance. It comes from nearness, his kindness, his patience, his fairness, his unparalleled knowledge, his eloquent speeches, his humility, his tenderness with the weak, and his refusal to lose himself even when the world around him was losing its way.

More than fourteen centuries ago, Imam Ali taught mankind that **every human being is either your brother in faith or your equal in humanity**. A sentence spoken long before the world imagined human rights. A sentence that tells us more about him than any battle or miracle ever could.

This book is not an attempt to praise him with exaggeration. His life does not need decoration. What he needs, and what humanity needs, is understanding, an honest, warm, human understanding of a man who lived truth so consistently that he defined its meaning for generations.

As the Apostle of Compassionate Leadership, I have spent years teaching leaders to rise above ego, to serve their people, to carry responsibility with dignity. But Imam Ali taught these principles before leadership became a science. He lived them before scholars wrote about them. He practiced them not as techniques, but as character.

This book is my journey into his humanity. It is an invitation to walk beside him as I share his story. It is an attempt to let modern readers see him as I came to see him, a noble man whose footsteps any sincere heart can attempt to follow, even if imperfectly.

If this book succeeds, even a little, every reader will put it down wishing to speak more gently, act more justly, think more clearly, defend truth more bravely, and live more compassionately.

If that happens, then the spirit of Imam Ali continues its work in this world. And that is all any writer could ever hope for.

The Child of the Sacred House

Imam Ali's life began with a sign so rare that it still astonishes historians and believers alike. He was born inside the Kaaba, the sanctuary that had been the center of devotion for centuries. No one before him, and no one after him, is known to have entered that sacred space at birth.

His mother, Fatima bint Asad, approached the Kaaba in labor. The doors were closed, and her pain was growing stronger. It is said that the walls opened for her by the will of God, and she entered alone. Days later, she emerged holding a child whose life would come to reshape the meaning of courage, truth, and justice.

His birth in that sanctuary felt symbolic even to those who later reflected on it. The man who would spend his life defending truth began his journey in a place built for the worship of the One. It was as if his life opened at the center of faith before it opened into the world.

Imam Ali's early childhood reflected that blessing. Before he learned to speak, before he lifted a sword, before history carved his name into memory, he lived in a home where mercy was practiced as naturally as breathing. His father, Abu Talib, was not a wealthy man, but he was a man of honor. He protected the Prophet Muhammad long before the message of Islam was revealed. His mother was known for her generosity, her devotion, and her warmth toward others. Their home was not filled with riches, but it was filled with dignity.

It was a household where kindness was not discussed as an idea. It was lived as a habit. But destiny had a different path waiting for the young Imam.

Mecca faced economic hardship, and his father, Abu Talib carried the burden of a large family. Muhammad, who was already known among his people for honesty and compassion, offered to help lighten the load. It was not charity. It was love between relatives who trusted each other. Imam Ali went to live under the care of the Prophet, entering a home that would shape his soul long before it shaped his destiny.

In that home, young Imam Ali saw a different kind of strength. He saw no arrogance, no harshness, no cruelty. He watched the Prophet treat children with gentleness, neighbors with respect, the poor with generosity, and even strangers with dignity. These were not lessons taught through commands. They were lessons lived in everyday moments. Ali, the young child, absorbed them quietly, the way a young plant absorbs sunlight.

He learned that strength could be soft. And authority could be gentle. He learned that truth did not need loud voices to stand tall.

His childhood was marked by acts of kindness that felt instinctive. He shared food even when there was little. He cared for those younger than him. He followed the Prophet into prayer before he understood the depth of prayer. He stood beside truth before he knew the cost of standing there.

When the first revelation came, Imam Ali was still a boy. He recognized sincerity immediately. Some people later tried to describe his acceptance of Islam as youthful obedience. But I tell you, belief is not obedience. Belief is recognition. A pure heart recognizes purity, and Imam Ali's heart was clear.

He became the first child to embrace the new faith. He did not hesitate. He did not ask for proof. He was certain. He simply knew and believed.

That certainty was not sudden. It was formed in the environment he grew up in. He had watched the Prophet's honesty, his patience, his mercy. When the message came, it matched the man he had always known. There was no contradiction to question. Only truth to accept.

As the early days of Islam grew more difficult, Imam Ali remained close to the Prophet. He saw the mockery, the insults, and the cruelty directed at the small group of believers. He witnessed the pain, but he also witnessed the dignity with which the Prophet responded. He saw that real strength was not found in retaliation, but in restraint.

His years with the prophet were lessons no school could teach. They were lessons carved into the heart through daily example.

Imam Ali's character was being formed quietly. His compassion became the bedrock of his courage. His humility created space for wisdom. His simplicity protected him from arrogance. While other young men of his age were shaped by tribal pride and competition, Imam Ali was being shaped by mercy, truth, and devotion.

People later remembered Imam Ali for his bravery in battle, for his unmatched strength, for his eloquence, and for his judgments. But his true greatness began long before any battlefield or pulpit. It began in the quiet corners of early life. In the innocence of a child who chose kindness before he knew what power meant. In the heart of a boy who learned mercy before he learned strategy.

Greatness is not born in public moments. It is formed in private ones, when kindness is chosen over pride, when fairness is chosen over advantage, when empathy is chosen over ego. Imam Ali's humanity is reachable. It is a path any person can attempt to walk.

His birth was a sign. His childhood was preparation. His character became the foundation upon which truth would later stand. And the footsteps he left behind are human enough for every reader to follow.

The Man Who Loved Before He Led

Long before history knew him as a leader, Imam Ali was a man who loved with sincerity. His life did not begin in the arena of power. It began in the intimacy of family, in the quiet loyalty of friendship, and in the small responsibilities that shape a human heart long before they shape a public one.

To understand Imam Ali's greatness, one must understand the woman he married. Fatima was not only the daughter of the Prophet. She was the embodiment of dignity, compassion, and moral purity. Her presence filled her father's home with warmth and grace, and her loss later left a wound that history still feels.

If Mary is a symbol of holiness in Christianity, then Fatima holds a similar place in Islam. She was a woman whose purity and character touched every heart that encountered her. Her strength was quiet. Her dignity was natural. She did not seek admiration, yet admiration followed her.

Imam Ali married Lady Fatima through compatibility of spirit. They shared the same upbringing in the Prophet's household. They learned the same values, practiced the same humility, breathed the same compassion, and carried the same love for justice.

Their home was simple and humble. There was little to no furniture. The food was modest. Comfort was rare. Inside that small home was a kind of wealth the world cannot measure: respect, tenderness, partnership, and spiritual closeness. They did not compete. They completed each other.

Imam Ali helped with the chores. He ground grain. He fetched water. He carried supplies. He soothed the children when they cried. These were not the expected duties of a man in that era, but Imam Ali was not an ordinary man. For him, service was not humiliation. It was love expressed through action.

Fatima once felt the burden of the household labor weighing heavily on her hands. Imam Ali with all of his life duties quietly took on more of the burden. He rose earlier. He worked harder. He carried more of the physical strain so she would not feel alone. This was Imam Ali before the title of caliph, before the battles, before the politics. A man who valued the comfort of his wife more than the comfort of his own body.

With his children, Imam Ali was tender. Imam Hassan and Imam Hussein grew up in a home where both parents were present, emotionally engaged, and deeply loving. Imam Ali carried his sons on his shoulders. He played with them on the floor. He spoke to them with softness. He listened to them. He laughed with them.

He did not raise them through fear or authority. He raised them through example.

Children do not learn from commands. They learn from what they see. What they saw in Imam Ali was kindness expressed as strength, not softness mistaken for weakness. They saw a father who prayed at night, worked during the day, and still found time to sit with them in warmth and affection.

Imam Ali's love extended beyond his home. He cared for orphans with the same tenderness he gave his own children. His nights were often spent delivering food to widows, the elderly, and families who had no one to rely on. He did this quietly, without witnesses, without recognition.

He did not want praise. Nor attention. He wanted sincerity. Generosity performed in daylight is charity. Generosity performed when no one is looking is sincerity. Imam Ali preferred the second.

People admired his intellect, his courage, and his eloquence. But those who lived near him admired something deeper. They admired his ability to love without calculation. He loved the truth more than his ego. He loved his community more than his political right. He loved peace more than victory. He loved people more than he loved power.

That is why he rarely fought for authority, even when it was rightfully his. A man who values people more than himself does not rush toward thrones.

Imam Ali's character teaches a truth many leaders still fail to understand. Great leadership begins at home. If a man cannot be compassionate with the people closest to him, he will never be compassionate with the people he leads.

His love shaped him long before his leadership was tested. His tenderness formed the backbone of his strength. His humility became the foundation of his courage. Public leadership came later. The private discipline of love came first.

This is why the reader begins to admire him, not first as a warrior, not as a statesman, but as a human being whose heart was pure, whose motives were sincere, and whose actions matched the values he spoke about.

Imam Ali was a man who could lead armies yet lower himself to comfort a crying child. A man who could defeat giants in battle yet feel pain when a widow struggled to feed her family. A man who could stand firm against corruption yet speak softly to the poor. A man feared by enemies yet loved by the innocent.

This balance is rare. It is the kind of balance that makes a human being unforgettable. It is why, centuries later, hearts still turn toward him with admiration.

Imam Ali loved before he led. And because he loved, he led differently.

If you want to lead with justice, begin with compassion. If you want to speak with authority, begin with sincerity. If you want to influence others, begin by loving them.

His footsteps are not far from any of us. They begin with kindness.

The Home of Love and the Heart of Mercy

When Imam Ali returned home after long days of responsibility, the world often saw a leader, a warrior, a judge, a scholar, a man of unmatched courage and wisdom. But behind the doors of his modest home, he was something even greater. He was a devoted husband to Lady Fatima and a gentle, attentive father to Hasan, Husayn, Zaynab, and Umm Kulthum. In that home, titles disappeared. What remained was love.

The bond between Imam Ali and Fatima was not merely a marriage. It was a companionship of the soul. They shared the same upbringing under the Prophet, the same values, the same humility, and the same tenderness toward others. Their home was simple. Their possessions were few. There was little furniture, modest food, and almost no comfort. Yet their hearts were full.

They worked side by side, not as competitors, but as partners. They sacrificed comfort so others could eat. They shared responsibility without pride or complaint. Their home was built not on wealth, but on respect, patience, and spiritual closeness.

Fatima understood Imam Ali in a way few ever could. She knew the weight he carried, the expectations, the struggles, and the sacrifices he never spoke about. And he understood her gentleness, her strength, and her deep spiritual depth.

Their marriage was founded on mutual trust and faith strong enough to soften every hardship.

When the world misunderstood him, she understood him. When he felt pressure, she steadied him. When she suffered, he comforted her.

They were two hearts beating in harmony, each completing the other.

Their home became a sanctuary where their children grew not with privilege, but with values. Hasan, the eldest, inherited his father's composure and patience. He carried a calm wisdom even in moments of tension. Husayn inherited his father's courage and his unwavering commitment to justice. He carried a fire that refused to bow to oppression. Little Zaynab watched her father closely. She absorbed his strength, his clarity, his eloquence, and his dignity. From him she learned endurance, truthfulness, and grace in the face of hardship. These qualities would later define her in one of history's greatest trials.

Imam Ali did not raise his children through authority. He raised them through tenderness. He sat with them, taught them, listened to them, and spoke to them as if each one carried a universe inside. He was never too busy to kneel and tie a sandal, wipe a tear, or answer a question with care.

He planted in them the seeds of compassion, humility, and courage. He taught them that truth was a responsibility, not a weapon. That patience was strength, not weakness. That generosity was measured by the heart, not by wealth.

To Hasan, he passed the wisdom of leadership, the ability to remain calm in the middle of turmoil, to think before acting, and to forgive even when forgiveness was difficult. To Husayn, he passed the fire of conviction, the courage to stand alone, and the willingness to give everything for what is right. To Zaynab, he gave the depth of his heart, the strength to face tragedy, and the eloquence to speak truth when others fell silent.

Their home witnessed moments of laughter and moments of tears. Moments of comfort and moments of sacrifice. It was a home where compassion mattered more than wealth, where service mattered more than comfort, and where faith guided every decision.

But the love inside that home did not remain inside its walls.

Imam Ali carried the same tenderness into the streets, into the markets, into the homes of the poor and forgotten. He lived in a world where strength was worshipped, wealth defined status, and tribes measured a man's worth by the number of warriors behind him. He chose to define himself by something the world did not yet understand: mercy.

This was not mercy performed for attention. Not mercy that needed witnesses. Not mercy that waited for praise.

His was a quiet mercy, one that lived in the dark corners of the night where only God, hunger, and a man's conscience are awake.

From a young age, Imam Ali felt a deep responsibility toward those who had no one. He grew up watching the Prophet feed the hungry, shelter the stranger, and protect the vulnerable. These examples softened him even as they strengthened him. Compassion was not an ornament in his character. It was a discipline. It was how he understood the world.

He saw people not as tribes, but as God's creation. Not as rivals, but as humans. Not as numbers, but as responsibilities.

One of the most beautiful aspects of his character was the way he cared for orphans. Many leaders donate. Few leaders visit. He did both. He would kneel down to speak to children at eye level, wipe their tears, comfort them, and make sure they never felt abandoned. People later said that for many orphans in his city, the word "father" had a second meaning: Imam Ali.

He never gave from abundance. He gave from need. He shared bread when he himself was hungry. He gave coins until nothing remained in his hand. And he did not give to be thanked.

Once, he passed by a woman struggling to carry heavy water containers. She had no husband, no sons, no family to help her. Imam Ali, carrying the burdens of leadership, stepped forward, took the containers from her arms, and carried them to her home. She did not know who he was. She only saw a kind stranger.

The next morning, he returned with food. He continued helping her until she could manage on her own. Only later did neighbors tell her that the kind stranger was the leader of the entire Muslim community. She wept from embarrassment, but Imam Ali never mentioned it again.

That was his way. To be present. To help quietly. To ease burdens without speaking of his own.

At night, his compassion reached its purest form. He would disguise himself, carrying bags of flour, dates, and coins to families in need. He did this for years. No one knew it was him. Only after his death did the nighttime deliveries stop. Widows began asking, "Where is the man who used to knock on our door?" That man was Imam Ali.

His silence was his sincerity.

His compassion was not limited to the poor. It extended to the wronged and the marginalized, people ignored by society. He listened patiently to complaints from the poor, the enslaved, the elderly, and even those who disagreed with him politically. He never dismissed anyone. He did not see people as interruptions. He saw them as responsibilities.

As a judge, he investigated disputes with remarkable fairness. When a Jewish man accused him of taking his armor, he stood beside him in court as an equal. When the judge addressed Imam Ali by his title but not the other man by his name, Imam Ali corrected him. To him, justice could not exist if dignity was unbalanced, even in a single word.

In conflicts, he stood with the oppressed, not because it was politically safe, but because it was morally necessary. He believed that the true measure of a society was the condition of its weakest members.

Even in battle, where emotions run high and mercy is often abandoned, Imam Ali carried compassion with him. He never struck a wounded opponent. He never attacked a fleeing enemy. He never took pride in killing. His strength was guided by empathy.

War, for him, was not a place to unleash cruelty. It was a place to protect life when protection became unavoidable. He never lifted his sword unless he believed it was the last option. He avoided unnecessary bloodshed. He did not strike first. He never attacked the unarmed.

In a time when warriors sought glory, Imam Ali sought justice. In a time when power demanded fear, he offered dignity. In a time when strength was measured by domination, he measured it by mercy.

This chapter of his life teaches a simple truth: compassion is not weakness. It is a form of power that only rare souls know how to carry.

Imam Ali's compassion was not seasonal. Not conditional. Not selective. It was a way of existing. And this is where the reader begins to understand him, not through legends or poetry, but through the ordinary beauty of his humanity.

To understand Imam Ali, one must look at that small home he built with Fatima. A home where the husband honored the wife, where the wife supported the husband, where children were raised with values instead of privileges, and where love was expressed not through possessions, but through presence.

In that home, he was not the warrior. Not the Caliph. Not the judge. He was a husband, a father, a companion. And perhaps in those roles, he reached the highest expression of his humanity.

The Gentle Man in the Midst of War

War reveals a person's true nature. It strips away the polite language of peace, the safety of quiet homes, the comfort of routine. In war, a man either rises to protect life or sinks into the temptation of cruelty.

Imam Ali rose.

He lived in an era where battles were not distant events watched from screens. They were personal. They were hand-to-hand. They demanded courage, clarity, and moral steadiness. It would have been easy for a man of his strength to allow anger, pride, or power to shape his actions. But Imam Ali carried something into battle that most warriors left behind: **his humanity**.

People remember him as the lion of the battlefield, the warrior no opponent could defeat, the man whose presence changed the outcome of wars. But they often forget how he fought, **with restraint, not rage; with purpose, not cruelty; with clarity, not vengeance**.

Imam Ali never lifted his sword unless he believed it was the last option to protect truth, the vulnerable, or the unity of the community. He avoided unnecessary bloodshed. He did not strike first. He never attacked the unarmed. And he refused to celebrate victory over another human being.

He once said:

"Victory is not in defeating an enemy. Victory is in defeating your anger."

This was his philosophy in battle.

In the Battle of Badr, Uhud, the Trench, and Khaybar, his courage was unmatched, but so was his self-control. The people around him could not understand how a man so powerful could remain so gentle. Yet this contradiction was the essence of who he was: a warrior in physical strength, a servant in moral purpose.

One of the most famous moments of his life happened in the heat of battle. Imam Ali had disarmed an opponent and was moments away from delivering the final blow. In desperation, the defeated man spat in Imam Ali's face. A lesser man would have responded with fury. A lesser man would have struck immediately to defend pride. But Imam Ali stepped back, lowered his sword, and walked away.

His enemy stared in confusion. Why would a warrior spare a man who insulted him?

Imam Ali simply said:

"I fight only for the sake of Allah (God) and for justice. Your insult tempted my anger. If I struck you in that moment, it would have been for myself, not for truth."

Who thinks like this in war?

Who has that level of control when adrenaline fills the veins and death stands inches away?

A man whose heart guides his sword, not the other way around.

Imam Ali even treated his opponents as human beings. After battles, he ensured the injured were cared for, regardless of which side they fought on. He forbade mutilation. He forbade humiliation. He forbade cruelty. He protected the dignity of the defeated.

And when war ended, the sword returned to its sheath as if it had never tasted battle at all.

The people marveled at his bravery, but it was his restraint that defined him. Anyone can fight. Few can stop themselves from fighting when provoked. Imam Ali did both, he rose when justice required it and stepped back when ego whispered for attention.

During the civil wars that tore the Muslim community apart, the Battles of Jamal and Siffin, Imam Ali carried sorrow heavier than armor. He was not fighting enemies; he was facing Muslims who had been misled by ambition, fear, or manipulation. Every strike in those wars broke his heart. He often said that the worst pain a leader can feel is the pain of fighting those he wishes to protect.

In the chaos of battle, he would call out loudly for people to stop, reconcile, reflect. He tried to prevent bloodshed at every turn.

He sent envoys, letters, and pleas. He offered peace again and again, even when others accused him of weakness for doing so.

But Imam Ali understood something few leaders understand:

Peace offered sincerely is not weakness. It is strength in its highest form.

He fought only when he had no other choice left. And even then, he fought with a shattered heart.

His sword was sharp, but his conscience was sharper. His courage was vast, but his compassion was deeper. His victories were many, but his mercy was greater than them all.

Any person can pick up a weapon. Few can hold one without losing themselves. Imam Ali's greatness was not in the wars he won, it was in the humanity he refused to lose.

This is the kind of leadership the world still aches for. And it is the kind of example that makes every reader wish to walk as he walked, even in the storms of life, with dignity, restraint, and a heart that refuses cruelty.

Justice as an Act of Humanity

Justice, for many leaders, is an idea they speak about in speeches or write into laws. For Imam Ali, it was a responsibility that lived inside him. It shaped his decisions, guided his judgments, and influenced the way he treated every human being who stood before him. It was not a slogan, not a performance, and not a tool used to protect power. It was the purest reflection of his character.

He did not treat justice as a rigid legal structure. He treated it as compassion guided by clarity. To him, justice was not about punishment or domination. It was about protecting dignity. It was about making sure the weak were not crushed by the strong, and the voiceless were not ignored by those in authority.

He lived in a time when leaders favored their clans, rewarded their allies, and often ignored corruption if it came from someone influential. Tribal loyalty was stronger than moral responsibility, and power was often used to shield the privileged. Imam Ali refused to participate in that system. He would not give advantage to anyone simply because they were close to him. He would not excuse wrongdoing because of wealth, status, or personal loyalty. And he would never bend the truth to make his leadership easier. He feared only one thing: injustice.

He believed that justice was the foundation upon which life

itself stands. When justice collapses, everything else eventually follows. Wealth cannot hold a society together. Power cannot. Fear cannot. Only justice can create the trust that allows people to live in peace with one another.

He once expressed the idea that a society may survive disbelief, but it will not survive injustice. He understood that injustice spreads quietly, like poison in the bloodstream. It weakens trust, divides people, and slowly destroys the moral structure of a nation. So he confronted injustice with fairness, not with anger. With clarity, not with force.

One of the most remarkable moments of his life took place in a courtroom. A Jewish man claimed ownership of a shield that was in Imam Ali's possession. At that time, Imam Ali was the caliph, the leader of the Muslim world. Yet he walked into the court not as a ruler, but as a citizen standing before the law.

When the judge addressed him by his title but did not address the Jewish man with equal dignity, Imam Ali corrected him. He believed that justice cannot stand on uneven ground. In a court of law, titles must disappear and equality must take their place.

The judge asked Imam Ali for evidence. He had none.

So the judge ruled against him. The caliph lost the case.

The Jewish man stood there in shock. He had never witnessed such a moment. A ruler judged against himself, by a judge he himself had appointed, and in favor of a man from another faith. This was not the justice of kings or conquerors. It was the justice of conscience. That moment alone moved the man deeply, not because Imam Ali preached to him, but because Imam Ali lived what he believed.

Imam Ali did not see justice as a system of punishment. He saw it as a form of protection. It protected the weak from being crushed. It protected the poor from being ignored. It protected the stranger from being mistreated. It protected even the enemy, as long as that enemy remained a human being with dignity.

He once reminded his governors that people have weaknesses, and a leader's role is to correct those weaknesses, not to crush the people who carry them. This belief shaped every decision he made, every appointment he approved, and every instruction he gave.

When he appointed Malik al-Ashtar as governor of Egypt, he wrote a letter that remains one of the most beautiful documents in the history of leadership. It was not written as an order from a ruler to a subordinate. It read more like advice from a father to a son, filled with moral clarity and human concern.

He instructed him to be a shelter for the weak and a source of comfort for the people. He warned him never to raise his voice in arrogance, never to favor the wealthy over the poor, and never to let anger guide his decisions. He reminded him to forgive whenever forgiveness protected dignity, and to avoid punishment whenever patience could repair a situation. He advised him to keep his doors open to the people, to beware of advisors who lacked conscience, and to sit with the poor as naturally as he sat with the powerful.

Above all, he reminded him of a principle that defines his entire philosophy of leadership: people are of two kinds, either your brothers in faith or your equals in humanity.

This was not a slogan written for history. It was the foundation of his leadership. Centuries before the language of human rights emerged, Imam Ali was already speaking the language of human dignity.

He believed justice begins in the heart before it reaches the court. A restless and arrogant heart produces injustice, no matter how perfect the laws may appear. A calm and fair heart creates trust, even in difficult circumstances. He taught that punishment should always be the last option, not the first. That reason must guide anger. That strength must be guided by fairness. And that dignity belongs to every human being, even the one who has done wrong.

He once expressed the idea that the best form of justice is the kind that protects the dignity of both sides. This was the balance he sought in every judgment he made. His justice was not cold or mechanical. It was warm, human, and deeply aware of the fragile nature of the human soul.

The Humility of a Noble Heart

Many leaders are remembered for their victories, their speeches, or the power they once held. But the deeper measure of a human being is often found in something less visible: the ability to remain humble, to speak honestly about one's limits, and to place truth above pride. This is where Imam Ali stands apart from most figures in history.

What made him extraordinary was not only his courage, his knowledge, or his sense of justice. It was the humility that lived within him, a sincerity so natural that it shaped the way he spoke, listened, judged, and led. He never claimed perfection, even though his life showed a level of clarity that few could match. His decisions were guided by principle, and those principles protected him from the kinds of mistakes that often come from ego, haste, or ambition.

Imam Ali never built his leadership on the idea that he was above others. He understood the limits of human beings, and he spoke about himself with the honesty of someone who feared arrogance more than criticism. He once expressed that he did not consider himself free from error, nor did he deny the possibility of being wrong. For a man

known for his intelligence and moral clarity, these words carried great meaning. He could have claimed certainty in all things, and many would have believed him. But he refused to create that illusion.

His honesty did not come from weakness. It came from integrity. Even those who opposed him admitted that there was hardly a question he could not answer. His understanding of law, faith, and human character was widely respected. Yet he never allowed knowledge to turn into pride. When people came to him with difficult questions, he answered when he knew. When he did not know, he simply said so.

He did not fear those words. He feared dishonesty more than he feared appearing limited. To him, truth mattered more than reputation. A leader who pretends to know everything eventually loses the trust of the people and the guidance of his own conscience.

On one occasion, people gathered around him, praising him in ways that suggested he was beyond human weakness. He stopped them and reminded them that he was a man like them. If he did right, they should support him. If he did wrong, they should correct him. This was not a display of modesty for the sake of appearances. It was a principle. He did not want followers who flattered him. He wanted people who remained loyal to truth, even if that truth required questioning their leader.

His humility was not the humility of confusion. It was the humility of a man who understood his responsibilities and carried them with care. When he paused before making a decision, it was not because he doubted himself. It was because he knew that every judgment could affect many lives. Leadership, in his eyes, was a trust, and a trust required thoughtfulness.

During the painful years of civil conflict, when he saw Muslims fighting one another, his heart carried the weight of that division. He spoke of his sorrow, because he saw how far people had drifted from the justice he offered. His sadness came from witnessing a community torn apart by ambition, fear, and misunderstanding.

Despite his powerful position, Imam Ali lived among the people without distance. He walked without guards, sat among ordinary citizens, and listened to complaints without barriers or ceremony. He did not surround himself with symbols of authority. He believed that every person, especially the weakest, deserved to be heard with dignity.

This made him approachable. People did not fear speaking to him. Even those who had done wrong knew that he would listen before judging, guide before condemning, and forgive when forgiveness was possible. His humility did not reduce his authority. It strengthened it. People trusted him because they felt seen and respected.

When conspiracies formed and betrayals occurred, he did not rush to anger or revenge. Instead, he examined himself first. Not because he believed he was always at fault, but because he believed a leader must begin with self-accountability. He asked whether he had communicated clearly, whether he had guided people enough, or whether he had expected more from them than they were ready to give.

This was not self-blame. It was compassion. He tried to understand the people's circumstances, their upbringing, and the influences that shaped their decisions. His heart was wide enough to carry the burdens of others without becoming bitter.

Imam Ali's humility was not a strategy or a political posture. It was the natural expression of a soul that had overcome its ego. His strength came from clarity. His authority came from righteousness. His leadership came from a heart disciplined by faith.

He taught that the most complete human being is the one who is most willing to correct himself. He lived this teaching without announcement. His reflections were personal. His self-corrections were sincere. He did not seek admiration for them. He did them to remain truthful.

For the modern reader, this is what makes him both admirable and relatable. People cannot easily connect with perfection that feels distant or unreachable. But they can connect with a leader who carries greatness without arrogance, authority without harshness, and wisdom without superiority.

Imam Ali was such a man. He moved through the world with a heart free from pride, a mind untouched by deception, and a character that remained steady even when the world around him was shaken by conflict.

His honesty was not the honesty of public confessions or dramatic admissions. It was the honesty of a man who understood that only God is perfect, and that human greatness lies in sincerity, humility, and the constant effort to remain true to what is right.

This was the humility that defined him, the humility of a noble heart, and it is one of the reasons his life continues to speak to people across centuries.

His Grief, His Fears, and the Depth of His Silence

A man may stand fearless on the battlefield, yet even the strongest heart carries wounds that no one sees. Imam Ali was no exception. His courage in public did not erase the sorrows he endured in private. Behind the strength that history remembers was a depth of feeling that only a few men have ever carried with such dignity.

His life was marked by losses that would have broken many others. He buried people he loved with the same hands that once lifted a sword in defense of truth. But when those hands lowered a loved one into the ground, his strength took on a different form. It was no longer the strength of battle. It was the strength of endurance, the ability to carry pain without allowing it to poison the heart.

The greatest sorrow of his life was the loss of Fatima. She was not only his wife. She was his companion in purity, the mother of his children, the daughter of the Prophet, and the light of his home. Their bond was built on shared values, mutual respect, and a deep understanding of the responsibilities they carried together. When she fell ill and passed away, something within him changed forever. The world outside continued to move, but inside him, a part of life slowed down and never fully returned to its earlier warmth.

Those close to him said that he often visited her grave alone. He would speak to her as if she were still listening, as if her presence continued to give him comfort. He was not a man who cried in public or sought sympathy from others. His grief was contained, dignified, and deeply human. He carried it the way he carried everything else in life, with patience and sincerity.

Leadership brought him another form of sorrow. He watched people he loved drift away from him. He saw companions misled by ambition, tribes influenced by politics, and friends who once stood beside him become distant when truth required sacrifice. Each betrayal left a mark, not on his convictions, but on his heart. He cared too deeply about people to harden himself against them, yet he felt the weight of their absence.

There were nights when he walked alone, not as a ruler, but as a man searching for peace in prayer. His supplications revealed fears he never spoke about in public. They were not fears for his own life. He had faced death too many times to fear it. What troubled him was the condition of the community. He feared a society drifting away from justice, children growing up without guidance, and truth becoming lost in the noise of ambition and politics.

His silence was never a sign of weakness. It was a form of wisdom. He often chose silence not because he lacked words, but because he understood that some truths must be spoken at the right time, in the right way, and to hearts prepared to receive them. He once said that the heart has moments of openness and moments of closure, and he lived by that understanding. When silence taught more than speech, he remained silent. When patience carried more dignity than confrontation, he chose patience.

Even in war, this depth of feeling was visible. Soldiers around him spoke of the expression in his eyes before battle. It was not fear. It was the sadness of a man who knew that every sword raised was a sign that human hearts had failed to choose peace. He fought only when there was no other option, and even then, he refused cruelty, revenge, or dishonor.

His fears were never for himself. He feared injustice spreading through society. He feared children growing up without moral guidance. He feared orphans being neglected, the poor being forgotten, and the weak being crushed by the strong. His fears were the fears of a leader who loved humanity more than he loved victory.

As his life neared its end, those around him noticed a change. He spent more time in reflection, more time in prayer, as if he sensed that his journey was approaching its final turn. His last nights in the mosque of Kufa were filled with devotion and contemplation.

When he was struck during the dawn prayer, his words revealed the peace he carried beneath years of sorrow. He said, in meaning, "By the Lord of the Kaaba, I have succeeded." These were not the words of a man escaping pain. They were the words of a man who felt he had fulfilled his trust, a man returning to the One whose presence he had felt in every moment of hardship.

This part of Imam Ali's life reveals something that deepens admiration for him. He endured heartbreak without losing compassion. He carried grief without losing clarity. He lived with fears without losing courage. And he embraced silence when silence was the most truthful response.

In his private struggles, Imam Ali becomes even more noble. And in that nobility, the reader feels closer to him, not only respecting him, but wishing to learn how to carry pain with the same dignity and grace.

The Courage That Spoke Truth

There are men who show courage only in battle, and there are men whose courage lives in the way they think, speak, and carry themselves each day. Imam Ali belonged to the second kind. His bravery did not begin with the sword, and it did not end there. It began in his heart, moved into his words, and shaped the way he lived among people who were not always comfortable with the truth he represented.

His courage was steady and grounded. It did not depend on noise, applause, or dramatic gestures. It came from a certainty that truth must be spoken, even when it is uncomfortable, and that silence in the face of wrongdoing only gives injustice more space to grow.

Imam Ali was known as a man who could stand among powerful figures and speak with calm honesty. He did not adjust his words to please those around him. He did not measure his speech by the approval of the crowd. He measured it by justice. If something needed to be said, he said it with dignity, without anger, without fear, and without calculation.

People listened to him not because he demanded their attention, but because his words carried conviction. Even those who disagreed with him recognized the weight behind what he said. His voice did not carry arrogance. It carried responsibility. When Imam Ali spoke, people felt that truth itself had found a mouth.

He grew up in the household of the Prophet, and that home shaped him. It did not only teach him revelation and worship. It taught him courage, the courage to stand against falsehood, even if standing alone. From a young age, Imam Ali absorbed this strength. Before he ever led armies, he led with truth. Before he ever held political authority, he carried moral authority.

He did not fear the consequences of speaking honestly. There were many moments when silence would have been easier, politically safer, and more convenient. He chose clarity. Corrected leaders when they strayed. Advised governors when they forgot their duties. He confronted injustice wherever he saw it. His voice did not rise out of anger. It rose out of principle.

In times of crisis, when people were confused and emotions ran high, Imam Ali's words often steadied the situation. After the passing of the Prophet, when fear and uncertainty filled the community, he spoke with wisdom instead of panic. He did not chase power. He focused on preserving unity and protecting truth. Even when he disagreed with others, he remained composed. Fairness shaped his tone, and patience guided his response.

His courage was deeply connected to his compassion. He did not speak out to prove himself right. He spoke because he cared about the people around him. He could not watch injustice harm the innocent and remain silent. To him, silence in the face of oppression was a form of participation in it. This belief shaped the way he lived and the way he spoke.

On the battlefield, his bravery was well known. Yet even there, his actions were guided by restraint and wisdom. He entered battles with a clear conscience, not with hatred or pride. He did not seek victory for himself. He sought justice for others. The same heart that spoke truth in councils was the heart that held the sword in defense of the weak.

Still, his greatest courage was not always seen in moments of war. It was seen in the way he confronted the moral weaknesses of society. He spoke about fairness when favoritism was common. He defended the rights of the poor when the wealthy expected privilege. He reminded those in power of their duties when ambition tempted them to forget the vulnerable. He believed that justice could not survive unless someone had the courage to defend it.

Even his moments of silence required courage. When he felt that people were not ready to hear certain truths, he chose patience instead of argument. He did not force wisdom into hearts that were closed. He waited, preserving unity when his words might have deepened division. This kind of restraint demanded as much courage as speaking out.

Imam Ali lived in a time when speaking truth could cost a man his life, yet he did not hesitate. His voice carried clarity because it was rooted in justice. His courage was visible not only in conflict, but in the daily strength it takes to correct, to guide, to forgive, and to remain steady when the world around you is not.

For the reader, seeing Imam Ali in this light changes the meaning of courage. He is no longer only a warrior in distant battles. He becomes a guide whose bravery can be imitated, not with weapons, but with honesty, conviction, and integrity.

He was fearless in battle, but even more fearless in conscience. And it is this kind of courage, calm, dignified, and unwavering, that makes his footsteps not only admirable, but possible for others to follow.

The Father and the Friend

History remembers Imam Ali for his courage, his knowledge, and his sense of justice. But those who lived close to him, those who shared his home, walked beside him, or sat with him in ordinary moments, saw another side of him. They saw a man whose strength never erased his tenderness. In fact, his tenderness was part of what made him strong.

As a father, Imam Ali carried his children with a love that was patient and sincere. Hasan and Husayn did not grow up under the shadow of a distant warrior. They grew up beside a father who balanced discipline with affection, guidance with warmth. He taught them more through example than through command. His life was their lesson.

Reports from early Islamic tradition describe how he treated them with softness. He carried them on his shoulders, played with them, and gave them his full attention. Even when leadership and conflict demanded much of his time, he never allowed responsibility to turn him into a distant father. When he returned home, he returned as a parent first, not as a ruler.

His love for his daughters carried the same depth. He protected them with care and treated them with respect. In a society that often measured women by narrow standards, Imam Ali reflected the teachings he learned from the Prophet, who elevated the status of daughters and taught that their presence in a home was a blessing. Imam Ali carried that same spirit into his own household. His daughters grew up in an environment where dignity was natural, not something they had to demand.

As a husband, Imam Ali lived as a true partner to Lady Fatima. Their marriage was built on balance, understanding, and shared values. Both had grown up under the guidance of the Prophet, and both carried the same sense of responsibility toward God and humanity. Their home was simple, with few possessions, yet it was filled with warmth and mutual respect.

Historical accounts describe how Imam Ali helped with the tasks of daily life. He carried water, ground grain, and shared the responsibilities of the household. He did not see service to his family as something beneath him. To him, love was expressed through action. The home they built together was small in size but rich in meaning. It was a place shaped by faith, sacrifice, and affection.

After the passing of Lady Fatima, the absence she left behind was deeply felt. Many reports speak of the sorrow that settled over Imam Ali during that period. Their bond had been built on shared belief, hardship, and devotion. Losing her was not only the loss of a wife. It was the loss of a companion who understood him more deeply than most people ever could. Those close to him sensed that something in his home had changed. Faith remained, responsibility remained, but the warmth she brought into his life could not be replaced.

Beyond his role as a father and husband, Imam Ali was also a loyal friend. He was known among his companions as someone who listened carefully, advised sincerely, and stood by others without calculation. People came to him for counsel, for comfort, or simply for the presence of someone who treated them with respect.

He did not place himself above others. He sat among his companions as one of them. He shared in their laughter and stood with them in their grief. If someone was troubled, he helped as much as he could, often without drawing attention to his own efforts. If someone wronged him, he forgave easily. If someone needed guidance, he spoke honestly, but with care for the person's dignity.

Those who spent time around him felt a sense of ease. That feeling did not come from power or authority. It came from his character. He treated people as human beings first, not as followers, rivals, or tools of politics. He made people feel respected, and that respect created trust.

In his friendships, Imam Ali balanced honesty with compassion. He did not flatter, but he did not humiliate either. When he corrected someone, he did so in a way that preserved their dignity. To him, friendship was a trust, not a convenience. It carried responsibility.

This side of Imam Ali, the father, the husband, and the friend, allows the reader to see him not as a distant figure from history, but as a human being whose love, loyalty, and tenderness were as real as his courage and wisdom. It is in these close relationships that his character becomes most visible.

The greatness of a man is not measured only by how he leads

nations. It is also measured by how he treats those closest to him. In Imam Ali, love and leadership lived side by side, each strengthening the other. His companionship was not a duty. It was a natural reflection of who he was.

The Last Night: Humanity at Its Peak

The nights of Ramadan in Kufa were usually filled with prayer, reflection, and a gentle stillness that settled over the city after sunset. But during those final nights of Imam Ali's life, those close to him sensed a different atmosphere. There was a depth to his presence, a calm that felt almost like farewell, though he did not announce it.

He moved through his home with a composure that comforted those around him, but carried a certain gravity. His children noticed it first. There was extra warmth in the way he spoke to them, more patience in his tone, and longer pauses between his words. He spent time with each of them, giving attention and care, as if he wanted to leave them with the memory of his presence rather than the weight of his absence.

He had faced many battles in his life, but that night his strength appeared in another form. It was the strength of a man who had surrendered himself completely to God's will. There was no anxiety in him, no bitterness, no fear. His calm came from a life lived with sincerity, a life in which he had carried responsibility without losing his humanity.

Even during those final hours, his concern for others did not fade. He continued to think of the poor, the orphans, and those who depended on his support. Acts of care, small and ordinary, remained part of his routine. He did not seek grand gestures. He lived his final hours the same way he lived the rest of his life, with mercy toward those around him.

When he entered the mosque for the dawn prayer, nothing outwardly dramatic marked the moment. He walked as he always did, with humility and focus, preparing to stand before God. The mosque was quiet, the early hour still wrapped in darkness. For him, it was another moment of devotion, another step in a lifelong habit of prayer.

As he bowed his head in worship, the assassin struck. The blow was sudden, delivered while he was in prayer. Those nearby rushed toward him, shocked by what had just happened. In that moment of pain, his response reflected the spirit of his entire life. He is reported to have said, in meaning, “By the Lord of the Kaaba, I have succeeded.” It was not a cry of despair. It was the expression of a man who believed he had fulfilled his trust.

He was carried back to his home, wounded, while his family and companions gathered around him. Hasan held his hand. Husayn wept. The people of Kufa began to realize that they were losing not only a leader, but a moral anchor who had guided them through difficult times.

Even in that condition, his thoughts were not focused on revenge. He instructed his sons to treat the man who struck him with fairness. He asked that the attacker be given water and not be mistreated. If he survived, he said, he would decide the matter himself. If he did not, they were to act justly and not exceed the limits of the law. Mercy remained part of his character even in the face of death.

His final advice to his children reflected the values by which he had lived. He urged them to remain conscious of God, to uphold justice, to care for the poor, to protect the orphans, to speak the truth, and to preserve unity among people. He did not leave behind wealth or political instructions. He left principles, knowing that principles endure longer than power.

As his final moments approached, his voice grew weaker, but his composure remained. There was no panic, no bitterness. Those around him saw a man at peace with his life and ready to return to the One he had worshipped for so many years.

When he passed away, the loss was deeply felt. A leader had fallen, but more than that, a conscience had departed from the world. Yet his life left behind something stronger than grief. It left an example.

In his final night, one sees the essence of who he was. A father who comforted his children, a leader who refused cruelty even toward the one who attacked him, and a servant of God who met death with calm acceptance.

He did not meet his end as a man clinging to power. He met it as he had lived, as a servant of God, a father, a defender of justice, and a man whose heart remained open to mercy until his last breath.

Why His Humanity Outlives His Sword

History celebrates warriors. Statues rise for conquerors. Nations tell stories of victories, battles, and the men whose swords carved borders into the world. But Imam Ali did not become eternal because of the wars he fought or the enemies he defeated. He became eternal because of the way he lived, with tenderness, justice, courage, and a heart so open that it could hold the pains of a nation without bitterness.

When people speak of Imam Ali today, they do not speak of conquest. They speak of character. They remember the man who walked at night to feed the poor, who carried food on his back so no child would sleep hungry. They remember the leader who won a court case against himself and accepted the judgment with grace. They remember the father who played with his children on his shoulders. They remember the friend whose honesty lifted others, never humiliated them. They remember the husband who honored Fatima with a love that still inspires hearts centuries later.

Imam Ali's humanity became his legacy because it was inseparable from his soul. His courage was grounded in compassion. His leadership was inseparable from fairness. His wisdom grew from humility. Even his silence carried meaning, offering guidance when words were too heavy for the moment. He fought only when he had no choice, and even then, he fought with restraint, always conscious that the people in front of him were God's creation too.

A sword can win a battle. A heart like Imam Ali's can guide generations.

This is why his legacy endures. His greatness was not confined to the battlefield. It lived in the stories of the weak, the forgotten, the orphans, the widows, and the ordinary people who saw in him a reflection of the values they wished to live by. His influence did not depend on armies or power. It depended on example.

Those who opposed him in politics could not deny his integrity. Those who fought him in war could not deny his honor. Those who envied him could not deny his knowledge. And those who loved him knew that his presence made the world feel gentler, safer, and clearer.

Even today, when people discover his words, they find themselves surprised by how modern, how human, how deeply insightful they are. His sermons inspire thinkers. His letters guide leaders. His prayers soothe hearts. His sayings illuminate the path for those seeking meaning. It is as if he spoke not only to his time, but to the future, to every generation that would struggle with justice, identity, mortality, and truth.

He taught that strength means nothing if it lacks mercy. That knowledge means nothing if it lacks humility. That faith means nothing if it lacks justice. That leadership means nothing if it lacks compassion. And that a heart becomes noble only when it cares for others more than itself.

This is why Imam Ali is not remembered as a ruler, but as a conscience. Not as a warrior, but as a guide. Not as a man of power, but as a man of principle.

Nations forge heroes through myths. But Imam Ali needs no myth. His actions speak for themselves, actions so real, so consistent, and so sincere that they have become symbols of the highest human behavior.

His humanity outlives his sword because humanity is eternal. His justice outlives his battles because justice is universal. His compassion outlives his struggles because compassion is timeless. And his words outlive his life because truth does not die.

For every reader who turns these pages, Imam Ali becomes something personal, a mirror that shows the best version of who we can be. His footsteps do not demand perfection; they invite sincerity. His example does not require greatness; it inspires goodness.

And in that invitation, Imam Ali continues to walk beside humanity, long after his sword returned to its sheath, long after his voice fell silent, long after his body left this world. It is his heart, noble, pious, courageous, and endlessly compassionate, that remains.

The Standard of Truth

In every age, people search for truth. They argue over it, define it in different ways, and sometimes reshape it to suit their own desires. Across history, however, there are rare individuals whose lives become a measure by which truth itself is recognized. Imam Ali was one of those individuals. He was not simply a man who followed truth when it was convenient. His character reflected it so consistently that the Prophet is reported to have said that Ali stands with truth, and truth stands with Ali. This was not a title he claimed for himself. It was a quality people recognized in the way he lived.

His truthfulness did not change with circumstances, alliances, or outcomes. It did not bend for politics, nor did it soften for comfort. It came from a heart deeply connected to God, a mind that saw beyond illusions, and a soul that did not shift with public opinion. He remained the same whether he was supported or opposed, whether he stood among friends or critics.

His commitment to truth was not harsh or self-righteous. It was steady and clear. He spoke with the gentleness of someone who loved people and with the courage of someone who feared no one but God. When he corrected wrongdoing, he did so to elevate the person, not to humiliate them. When he exposed injustice, it was to protect those who could not protect themselves. He understood that silence in the face of falsehood often gives it strength, so he chose clarity over convenience.

People often approached him hoping he would support their decisions or defend their claims. If they were right, he stood beside them without hesitation. If they were wrong, he stood against them, even if they were his friends or supporters. He never tied his loyalty to people. He tied it to principle. His allegiance belonged to justice, fairness, and the dignity of the vulnerable, not to tribes or political interests.

Because of this, he became a reference point for moral judgment. People learned to ask themselves where Imam Ali stood on an issue. If he supported something, they saw it as righteous. If he opposed it, they understood that something within it required correction. His presence served as a moral compass during a time when the community was still learning to navigate life after the Prophet.

His dedication to truth brought comfort to the oppressed and discomfort to those who thrived on corruption. It also made his own path more difficult. Those who wanted a leader of convenience found him difficult to follow. Those who wanted a leader who could be influenced found him firm. Some desired unity at any cost, but Imam Ali believed that unity built on injustice cannot last. For him, truth was not something to negotiate.

He once spoke about how truth can leave a person with few companions. Even so, he did not abandon it. He accepted the loneliness that sometimes comes with integrity, because he believed that a leader who compromises truth even once may begin a pattern that leads to greater injustice. His firmness was not stubbornness. It was the discipline of a heart that understood the cost of moral compromise.

This clarity made him fearless. He spoke honestly to those in power and warned those who manipulated others for personal gain. He confronted injustice even when it cost him political advantage. He refused to flatter the powerful or ignore the weak. His truth was balanced. It carried strength without cruelty and clarity without arrogance.

Even those who opposed him could not accuse him of dishonesty. They may have disagreed with his decisions or feared his influence, but they recognized the sincerity behind his words. This consistency gave him a reputation that outlived his lifetime. People remembered him as a man whose voice carried fairness, whose actions reflected conscience, and whose character did not change with circumstance.

To follow Imam Ali is not simply to memorize his sayings. It is to measure ourselves against the standard he lived by. His life remains relevant because the struggle between truth and convenience continues in every generation. In a world where truth is often bent to serve power, his example reminds us that leadership is not about winning popularity. It is about standing for what is right, even when standing alone.

Imam Ali did not spend his life searching for truth as if it were something distant. He lived in a way that made truth visible. His words clarified it. His actions protected it. His character gave it form. And through that consistency, he became a standard that generations continue to look toward when they seek guidance.

His Human-Rights Leadership

Many rulers speak of justice. Many leaders claim to protect the weak. Governments throughout history have raised banners of law, order, and rights. But centuries before the world developed constitutions, before nations spoke of humanitarian principles, and long before international law began defining the treatment of civilians and prisoners, Imam Ali was already living, writing, and enforcing standards that many societies still struggle to achieve. His leadership offered a model of human dignity long before the modern language of human rights existed.

Imam Ali believed that the true test of power lies not in how a ruler treats loyal supporters, but in how he treats the vulnerable, the child, the widow, the prisoner, the stranger, and even the enemy who has laid down his weapon. In this understanding, his leadership rose above many of the rulers of his time and continues to stand apart even among those who came after him.

He taught his governors that leadership is not domination. It is guardianship and responsibility. It is service to every soul living under one's authority. When he appointed Malik al-Ashtar as governor of Egypt, he sent him a letter that remains one of the most remarkable documents of ethical governance. It was not a political instruction alone. It was a moral guide, written with the clarity of a statesman and the concern of a father.

In that letter, he advised him to become a source of comfort for the people, not a burden. He instructed him to rule with mercy rather than anger and to see the citizens not as subjects, but as human beings equal in dignity, whether they shared his faith or not. In one of the most widely quoted passages, he reminded him that people are either brothers in faith or equals in humanity. With these words, he expressed a principle that echoes through modern discussions of universal rights: that dignity does not come from tribe, religion, or political loyalty, but from the simple fact of being human.

He warned his governor not to raise his voice at the people, not to rule with harshness, and not to let anger guide his decisions. He encouraged forgiveness whenever possible and reminded him that power is a test rather than a privilege. A ruler, he wrote, must remember that God watches the hearts of leaders more closely than their public displays.

He also instructed his governors to live simply. They were to dress and eat like ordinary citizens, to walk among the people without arrogance, and to avoid the company of flatterers. He did not want rulers hidden behind palace walls or surrounded by praise. He wanted leaders who felt the hardships of their people and listened to them directly.

Corruption, in his view, was not limited to stolen money. It also included the theft of dignity, fairness, and hope. He warned that betraying public trust is the greatest form of treason, because it damages the spirit of a society before it damages its laws.

For judges, he laid out standards that were rare in his era. He ordered them to treat both sides in a dispute with equal respect. They were to greet them equally, listen to them equally, and judge them equally. No title, no wealth, and no social status could influence a decision. The court, in his understanding, was a place where every person stood on the same ground.

He practiced this principle in his own life. When he stood in court against a Jewish man over a shield, he did not use his position as caliph to demand special treatment. He stood as an equal before the judge. When the ruling went against him because of lack of evidence, he accepted it without protest. His acceptance of the judgment spoke more powerfully than any argument.

Even in war, Imam Ali maintained standards that reflected deep concern for human life. He instructed his soldiers not to harm women, children, or the elderly. He told them not to pursue a fleeing enemy or kill someone who had dropped his weapon. He forbade the destruction of homes, crops, and water sources. He prohibited torture, mutilation, and cruelty of any kind. For him, strength in battle did not justify the loss of moral restraint.

He insisted that prisoners of war be treated with dignity, fed the same food as their captors, and protected from abuse. In his eyes, a prisoner was no longer an enemy on the battlefield, but a human being under the protection of justice.

On one occasion, when a commander suggested harsh treatment for rebels, Imam Ali corrected him immediately.

He reminded him that these were people who had gone astray, not enemies to be destroyed. The goal, he explained, was not their blood, but their return to what was right. In this approach, he placed reconciliation above revenge and guidance above punishment.

Few rulers of his time spoke in this manner. Few generals placed such limits on their own power. His instructions were not political strategies designed to win favor. They were reflections of a heart that saw every person as a trust and every life as sacred.

Reading his letters today reveals how many of these concerns remain unresolved in the modern world. Societies still debate the treatment of prisoners, the rights of minorities, the dignity of the poor, and the ethics of warfare. Imam Ali addressed these matters with clarity and conscience, guided by a deep sense of moral responsibility.

What he left behind was more than a historical memory. It was a living example of how compassion and justice can shape leadership. The world often measures leaders by their achievements, their victories, or their influence. Imam Ali is remembered for something higher. He is remembered for the justice he demanded, the compassion he practiced, and the humanity he protected.

His life shows that leadership begins with the soul. A man who governs his own heart with honesty and discipline becomes a source of guidance for others. And when leadership grows from a purified heart, its influence continues long after titles and kingdoms disappear.

A Light That Refuses to Dim

His Legacy in Today's World

The life of Imam Ali did not end with his final breath, nor did his influence settle into the silence of his grave. Some people leave behind memories, others leave behind books or monuments, but a rare individual leaves behind a way of living, a compass so clear that generations continue to follow it long after the person himself has departed. Imam Ali became that kind of compass. Time has swept away empires, kings, armies, and monuments.

Entire civilizations have risen and disappeared, leaving behind little more than fragments of memory. Still, the voice of a man shaped by courage, justice, and compassion continues to travel across generations. The world has changed in its tools, its technologies, and its speed, but it has not changed in its deepest human needs. People still long for justice, still search for truth, still thirst for compassion. That is why his legacy endures. He spoke to the human soul, not merely to the politics of his era.

Civilizations have risen and fallen, and cultures have transformed in ways no one of his time could have imagined. Through all these changes, the values that defined him have remained both timeless and deeply relevant. His understanding of justice is still studied in academic settings. His sermons continue to be recited in places of worship. His

letters to governors are read by those who seek guidance in leadership. His prayers still offer comfort to people burdened by the struggles of daily life. His legacy cannot be measured by geography or era.

It is present in every region touched by his words and character, from North Africa to Iran, from the Middle East to South Asia, from universities to humble homes. Many who know little about the political conflicts of his time still recognize his sayings. Scholars from different traditions have studied his words and admired the clarity of his thought and the beauty of his language. Ordinary people facing hardship often find reassurance in the patience and wisdom reflected in his life.

His teachings on justice were not abstract ideas. They were principles he lived by. Leaders have quoted him when speaking about fairness. Judges have reflected on his rulings in their search for balance. Students of governance have examined his letters for ethical direction. Those concerned with the conduct of war have studied his instructions to soldiers as early examples of moral restraint in conflict. Across traditions, many thinkers have appreciated the depth of his reasoning and the universal tone of his message. More than a thousand years after his death, scholars and institutions have referred to his letter to Malik al-Ashtar as a model of just governance. It was written in a simple setting, by a man who did not rule from luxury or depend on elaborate bureaucracies. His guidance came from conscience, and conscience does not become outdated.

Still, the true strength of Imam Ali's legacy does not lie in institutions or academic recognition. It lives in the hearts of people. It appears in the way individuals learn to treat each other with fairness, in the courage to speak truth, in the instinct to protect the weak, and in the desire to live with sincerity. His life continues to answer questions that every generation must face. What is justice. What is leadership. How should the strong treat the vulnerable. What is the purpose of power. How does a person remain morally clean in a world filled with temptation.

He did not answer these questions with theories alone. He answered them through his life. He practiced justice in a society shaped by political struggle. He showed compassion in an environment that often rewarded harshness. He carried humility in a world that admired pride. He upheld fairness in a society divided by tribe and class. He lived with courage in a time filled with fear. Because he lived these values, they survived him.

In the modern world, leaders rise and fall with remarkable speed. Nations pursue stability while struggling under the weight of corruption, injustice, and inequality. Families look for guidance, communities seek fairness, and young people search for meaning in a world full of competing voices. In all these places, the teachings of Imam Ali return as a reminder of what leadership, morality, and humanity can look like when anchored in integrity. His life continues to serve as a measure, not because people study him out of obligation, but because his example answers questions that still trouble the world.

When a judge refuses to bend to pressure, when a court protects the weak from the powerful, or when a leader chooses fairness over favoritism, the spirit of his justice is present. He insisted that no one stands above the law, not even the ruler himself. That standard still challenges societies today. It appears wherever justice is treated as sacred, wherever fairness becomes more important than convenience or loyalty.

His compassion also lives in the quiet corners of the world. When a person feeds the poor without seeking attention, or when a volunteer gives time to help those in need, they follow a path he once walked. He served widows and orphans without revealing his identity, not out of secrecy, but out of sincerity. He believed goodness loses its purity when it becomes a performance. Every silent act of kindness in today's world carries something of that spirit.

In universities and classrooms, students search for wisdom that reaches beyond career success. They look for ways to understand themselves, their relationships, their responsibilities, and their purpose. Many of his words are studied in philosophy, leadership, and ethics because they speak directly to the human condition. His reflections on pride, humility, anger, patience, and self-discipline feel as relevant today as they did centuries ago. When a young person realizes that true strength lies in mastering the self, they are discovering a truth he taught long before psychology became a formal science.

Modern conversations about justice, human dignity, and ethical leadership also echo his principles. When activists stand against oppression, when communities demand fairness, or when institutions seek accountability, they walk along the path he once described. He warned leaders that the cries of the oppressed rise quickly, and that no society can endure when injustice weakens its foundation. His words continue to shape the moral language of movements that seek fairness in a complicated world.

Even in matters of conflict, his legacy remains visible. He taught that victory without dignity is a form of defeat, and that the strongest warrior is the one who restrains cruelty. Today, discussions about the ethics of war, the treatment of prisoners, and the protection of civilians reflect principles he lived centuries ago. His rules were not born from political theory but from a conscience that refused to abandon humanity, even in the harshest circumstances.

Imam Ali's influence also appears in the most ordinary moments of daily life. When a parent teaches a child to speak truthfully, when a friend offers sincere advice, when a person chooses forgiveness instead of retaliation, or when someone practices humility instead of pride, they are living the lessons he modeled. He taught that nobility is not found in grand gestures but in consistent goodness. That message remains as necessary today as it was in his own time.

Different people remember him in different ways. Some see him as a protector of orphans. Others see him as a source of knowledge. Many see him as a voice of justice. For millions, he remains a doorway to sincerity, faith, and moral strength.

His legacy continues because it speaks to something universal within the human being, the desire to be honest, to be fair, to be brave, and to care for others.

In every generation, people search for a model of greatness that does not corrupt, a form of authority that does not abuse, and a style of leadership that does not mislead. They look for someone who proves that strength and mercy can live in the same heart. Again and again, they find themselves drawn to Imam Ali, not because of the battles he fought, but because of the character he carried.

A sword may carve a path, but it cannot give direction to the soul. A kingdom may control territory, but it cannot command the human conscience. A monument may preserve a name, but it cannot preserve character. Only truth, compassion, courage, and sincerity travel across generations. Only a noble heart continues to influence people long after its owner is gone.

That is why his legacy does not fade. He remains what he was in his lifetime, a source of direction for those who feel lost, a standard for those who seek righteousness, and a reminder that true greatness is measured not by power, but by purity of character. A light that refuses to dim, a companion for the present, and a guide for the future.

The Night Destiny Knocked

The final chapter of Imam Ali's life unfolded during one of the most difficult periods in early Islamic history. The wounds left by the Battle of Ṣiffīn had not healed, and the arbitration that followed created confusion and anger among many people. Some believed the decision to accept arbitration was a compromise of divine judgment. Among them emerged a group later known as the Kharijites, men whose rigid understanding of religion left little space for the balance, patience, and wisdom that defined Imam Ali's leadership. What began as disagreement slowly turned into resentment, and resentment hardened into a plan.

On the nineteenth night of Ramadan, Imam Ali rose before dawn for the Fajr prayer in the Great Mosque of Kufa, just as he had done throughout his life. He moved without guards or ceremony. Those close to him later said he carried himself with a calm presence, as though he sensed that an important moment was approaching. Inside the mosque waited ʿAbd al-Rahman ibn Muljim al-Muradi. He concealed his intention behind the posture of a worshipper. His sword had been prepared for a single fatal strike.

As the prayer began, the assassin moved. When Imam Ali raised his head from prostration, the blade descended and struck his forehead. The wound was severe, and the poison on the sword spread quickly. People rushed forward in shock and panic, but Imam Ali's response revealed the depth of his faith. He uttered words that generations would repeat with awe: "By the Lord of the Kaaba, I have succeeded." In that moment, he spoke not as a victim of violence, but as a servant who believed he was returning to the One he had lived for.

The mosque filled with confusion and grief, but Imam Ali himself remained composed. He urged those around him not to react with cruelty or rage. He reminded them that justice must not be replaced by revenge, even in moments of deep pain. The man who had been struck was the same man who still called for fairness toward the one who struck him.

He was carried home, conscious but gravely wounded. Physicians examined him and realized the poison had spread through his body. They told him there would be no recovery, only the gradual closing of his life. For the next two days, he remained clear in his speech and steady in his heart. His sons, Imam Hasan and Imam Husayn, stayed at his side. Companions visited him, and crowds gathered outside the house, praying, and weeping. The atmosphere in Kufa was heavy with sorrow, but Imam Ali himself showed acceptance and calm.

During these final hours, he delivered his will to his sons, a message preserved across generations in both Sunni and Shia traditions. It remains one of the most powerful ethical statements in early Islamic history. His advice was simple, direct, and deeply human. He urged them to remain conscious of God in both public and private life, to stand with truth and justice, to care for the orphan and the poor, to maintain prayer and charity, to preserve family ties, and to protect the unity of the community. He warned them never to oppress anyone, reminding them that oppression becomes darkness in the hereafter.

Even with a wound still open on his head, he turned his attention to the man who had attacked him. His instructions to his sons revealed a level of justice that stunned everyone present. He ordered them to give the assassin food and water, to treat him without cruelty, and to avoid torture or mutilation. He told them that if he survived, he would decide the man's fate himself. If he died, they were to strike only once in return, no more than the blow he had received. It was the final expression of his lifelong commitment to justice, a justice untouched by anger or revenge.

On the twenty-first night of Ramadan, the end arrived quietly. His final words were filled with remembrance of God. He left the world in the same spirit with which he had lived, with clarity, dignity, and peace. His sons prepared his body for burial and carried out his instructions. He was buried at night, and the location of his grave was kept secret to protect it from political enemies. Only a small group witnessed the burial in the area known as al-Ghari, near present-day Najaf, a place that would later become one of the most visited sanctuaries in the Muslim world.

When morning came, Kufa felt the weight of a profound loss. A leader had died, but more than that, a moral voice had departed. People filled the streets in grief. Some repeated his sayings. Others remembered his fairness or his kindness. Many felt that the world itself had grown dimmer.

Still, Imam Ali did not leave behind only sorrow. He left a set of principles, clear, humane, and enduring, that continued to guide hearts long after his passing. His death did not close his legacy. It revealed its full meaning. A sword ended his life, but his words, his justice, and his humanity continued to live, carried from generation to generation by those who saw in him a model of what a human being could become.

A Man for All Humanity

When a life is lived with sincerity and moral clarity, it cannot remain confined to one nation, one tribe, or one school of thought. It reaches beyond its original setting and begins to speak to people who may not share the same language, religion, or culture. This is what happened with Imam Ali. He was born in the early days of Islam and lived through its most formative struggles, but his character did not remain limited to that era. His wisdom traveled across centuries, his ethics crossed cultures, and his courage spoke to people far removed from the world in which he lived. Over time, he came to be admired not only by Muslims, but by thoughtful individuals from many traditions who recognized in him a model of integrity, compassion, and moral strength.

Many who encounter his words today do so without first studying the details of his life. They may read a saying attributed to him in a book of wisdom, hear his name mentioned in a lecture on ethics, or come across a passage from his letters or sermons. Even without knowing the full story, they sense something uncommon in his voice. Scholars notice the clarity of his reasoning. Judges appreciate his commitment to fairness. Writers and poets admire the depth of his expression. Ordinary readers recognize in his words the concerns and struggles of their own lives. This broad appeal is not the result of legend or exaggeration. It comes from the consistency of a man whose actions matched his principles.

His life offers answers to questions that are not limited to one time or place. Every human being, at some point, faces the pressure to compromise values for comfort or advantage. Every person must decide how to respond to anger, injustice, or the temptation of power. The questions that shaped Imam Ali's decisions are the same questions that shape lives today.

How does one remain principled when others choose convenience over truth? How does a person stay humble when authority or recognition comes their way? How does one respond to wrongdoing without becoming unjust in return? How can someone defend the weak while knowing it may come at a personal cost? Imam Ali's life became a practical answer to these questions, not through abstract theory, but through lived example.

He showed that leadership is not a matter of control, but of responsibility. He demonstrated that real strength is measured by steadiness of character, not by displays of power. He proved that knowledge has value only when it leads to fairness and sound judgment. He taught that faith is not limited to ritual acts, but must appear in the way a person treats others, especially in moments of difficulty.

As the centuries passed, different cultures found different aspects of his character to admire. In Arab lands, he became known for his eloquence, courage, and devotion. In Persian tradition, he was honored for his spirituality and sense of justice. In South Asia, stories about his chivalry and compassion became part of popular memory. In Western writings on ethics and leadership, his sayings appear as examples of moral reasoning and principled governance.

Each culture saw in him something familiar, because the values he represented were not bound to a single society. They were rooted in what human beings everywhere recognize as noble.

What made him universal was not the political context in which he lived, but the character he carried through that context. His values did not depend on tribe, wealth, or status. They were grounded in the dignity of the human being. A fair judge in any century could recognize the justice in his decisions. A reformer in any country could see in him a companion in spirit. A parent raising children could look to his example when teaching honesty, patience, and compassion.

Imam Ali's life also showed that greatness does not depend on material display. He lived simply, wore modest clothing, and walked among ordinary people without barriers. He defended the weak, forgave those who wronged him, and insisted on justice even when it cost him the loyalty of powerful supporters. His strength came from a conscience shaped by faith and guided by principle.

Among his most well-known statements is the line, "People are of two types: either your brothers in faith or your equals in humanity." With this single sentence, he expressed an understanding of human dignity that still resonates today. It reminds readers that respect and fairness are not limited to those who share one's beliefs, but extend to every person simply because they are human.

Different groups remember him in different ways. To many Muslims, he is a righteous successor and a model of piety. To Shia Muslims, he is the rightful Imam and spiritual guide. To historians, he stands as a reformer who tried to build a just society in a time of turmoil. To philosophers, he represents moral reasoning shaped by conscience. To poets, he appears as a symbol of purity and courage. To the oppressed, he remains a champion of justice. To seekers of truth, he offers a mirror of sincerity.

His life continues to inspire because it reflects a standard that many people wish they could reach. He lived with courage, clarity, compassion, and a conscience that bowed only to God. His story invites readers not only to admire him, but to examine their own lives and choices.

Imam Ali did not belong to one community alone. He belonged to all who seek righteousness. He belonged to every heart that wishes to rise above anger, greed, and injustice. He belonged to every soul searching for a path that honors both God and humanity. This is why his name continues to be spoken with respect across generations. His life did not end with his passing. It lives on wherever people choose justice over convenience, mercy over revenge, and truth over comfort. In that sense, he remains what he has always been, a man for all humanity.

A Light That Teaches Beyond Time

Some leaders are remembered for the battles they fought. Others are remembered for the positions they held or the victories they claimed. A rare few are remembered for the words they left behind, words that continue to guide people long after the sound of their voices has faded. Imam Ali belongs to this rare group. His wisdom did not come from academic institutions or formal systems of philosophy. It came from a life shaped by revelation, struggle, service, and reflection. His words were not crafted for display or debate. They were spoken from experience, from a heart that understood both the strength and the weakness of the human soul.

Across centuries, his sayings have been preserved in the historical and literary traditions of both Sunni and Shia communities. They appear in sermons, letters, short maxims, and recorded conversations. Together, they form one of the richest bodies of moral guidance left by any figure in history. These sayings do not belong only to one time or one people. They speak to the conscience of every reader who encounters them, whether that reader is a scholar, a leader, a parent, or a young person searching for direction.

Among his most famous teachings is a line that captures the breadth of his vision: “People are of two types: your brothers in faith, or your equals in humanity.” With this single sentence, Imam Ali expressed a moral understanding that remains relevant in every age. He did not divide humanity into enemies and allies, or believers and outsiders. He reduced the human condition to two relationships, both worthy of respect. Either a person shares your faith, or they share your humanity. In both cases, dignity is required. This teaching stands as one of the clearest expressions of universal ethics in early history.

His sayings on justice reveal how central fairness was to his thinking. He once said, “Justice puts everything in its proper place.” This was not an abstract definition. It reflected how he governed and judged. Justice, in his view, was not about punishment or control. It was about balance, about ensuring that every person, every right, and every responsibility found its proper position. When justice disappears, confusion follows, and society begins to fracture. This understanding shaped his decisions, even when those decisions cost him political support.

On the subject of knowledge, Imam Ali spoke with a clarity that still resonates with students and scholars. He said, “The worth of a person is in what he knows.” He did not mean that knowledge should become a source of pride. For him, knowledge was a form of responsibility. The more a person understands, the more they are expected to act with wisdom and fairness. Knowledge without character, in his view, was an empty possession.

Although he was known for his bravery in battle, his understanding of courage was far deeper than physical strength. He said, “The bravest heart is the one that forgives.” This teaching shows how he measured strength. For him, courage was not about overpowering an opponent. It was about mastering one's own anger, rising above the desire for revenge, and choosing mercy when one had the power to harm.

When speaking about leadership, he described it as a moral duty rather than a privilege. He said, "A leader is the guardian of those he leads." In this short sentence, he summarized an entire philosophy of governance. Leadership, to him, was not about authority or prestige. It was about protection, responsibility, and service. The leader stands as a caretaker, not as a master.

His views on wealth were shaped by his own simple lifestyle. He lived modestly even when he held the highest office. He taught, "Contentment is a treasure that never ends." This statement reflects a deep understanding of human desire. Wealth, in itself, does not satisfy the heart. A person who is content carries a treasure that cannot be stolen, taxed, or lost.

Truthfulness occupied a central place in his teachings. He advised, "Say the truth even if it is bitter." This was not an easy principle to live by, especially in political life, where compromise and convenience often shape decisions. Yet he held to this standard, even when it cost him allies and influence. To him, a truth that causes discomfort is still better than a lie that brings temporary peace.

His teachings on mercy reveal the depth of his character. He said, "Show mercy to others, and God will show mercy to you." This was not a sentimental phrase. It reflected how he treated prisoners, opponents, and even the man who struck him in the mosque. Mercy, in his life, was not an emotion. It was a discipline.

Imam Ali also spoke often about self-discipline and the inner struggle of the human being. He said, "Your soul is like a precious jewel, discipline it with good character." In this image, he described the soul as something valuable that must be protected and refined. Without discipline, it becomes clouded. With good character, it begins to shine.

Patience was another theme that appeared frequently in his words. He taught, "Patience is of two kinds: patience over what hurts you, and patience from what tempts you." This distinction reveals a deep understanding of human struggle. Some trials come from pain and hardship, while others come from desire and temptation. Both require strength of character.

In matters of friendship, he valued honesty above comfort. He said, "Your true friend is the one who tells you the truth, not the one who agrees with you." In this teaching, he warned against the comfort of flattery. A real friend, in his view, is someone who protects your character, even if that protection comes in the form of difficult advice.

When speaking about the nature of the world, he reminded people not to become lost in its distractions. He said, "This world is a passing shadow, prepare for what lasts." His intention was not to lead people into despair, but to give them perspective. Life is temporary, and the choices made within it carry lasting consequences.

These sayings have survived not because they were collected in libraries, but because they were carried in the hearts of people who found truth in them. A student finds guidance in them when facing confusion. A leader finds responsibility in them when tempted by power. A parent finds tenderness in them when raising children. A person in pain finds comfort in them during hardship.

This is why his wisdom continues to live. His words are not tied to one century or one culture. They speak to the permanent questions of the human soul. Empires have risen and fallen since his time, languages have changed, and societies have transformed. His sayings remain clear and relevant, as if they were spoken for every generation.

Imam Ali's wisdom was not meant for a select group of followers. It was a gift offered to anyone willing to listen. His words still carry light, and that light continues to guide those who seek clarity, fairness, and sincerity in their lives.

His Speeches:

Windows Into the Soul of a Noble Leader

Great leaders are often remembered for the buildings they raised, the lands they ruled, or the victories they claimed. Extraordinary leaders are remembered for something deeper. They are remembered for the words they spoke and the meaning those words carried. Imam Ali belongs to this second group. His speeches were not political performances or ceremonial declarations. They were reflections of his inner life, windows into a mind formed by wisdom and a heart shaped by faith, struggle, and responsibility.

His sermons, letters, and public addresses have been preserved in historical collections, most famously in *Nahj al-Balāgha*. These texts do not read like the speeches of rulers seeking approval. They read like the reflections of a man who understood the weight of leadership and the fragility of the human soul. In them, he speaks about justice, the nature of the world, the duties of leaders, and the moral path every person must walk.

One of his most powerful teachings on justice appears in a sermon where he explains its role in society. He states that justice places everything in its proper position and stands as the strongest pillar of governance. In his understanding, justice is not limited to courtrooms or punishments. It is the structure that keeps a society balanced before corruption even has a chance to grow. It protects the weak from the powerful and prevents authority from becoming abuse. When justice exists, order follows naturally. When it disappears, even the most generous acts cannot repair the damage. In this vision, justice becomes the foundation of leadership itself, not a tool used after problems appear, but a principle that prevents those problems from forming.

In another sermon, he speaks about the nature of the material world. He describes it as a temporary dwelling that can deceive those who trust it too deeply. He warns that the world disappoints those who seek permanent comfort within it. His words are not meant to condemn life or deny its beauty. They are meant to clarify its purpose. He reminds his listeners that the world is a passage, not a final destination. A person who builds their identity on wealth, status, or public praise will eventually feel the emptiness of those things. Peace arrives when a person understands the temporary nature of worldly success and focuses instead on character, service, and sincerity. His message offers balance rather than rejection. Live in the world, he teaches, but do not allow the world to own your heart.

Perhaps his most famous address on leadership appears in his letter to Malik al-Ashtar, whom he appointed as governor of Egypt. In this letter, he outlines a complete vision of ethical governance. He instructs his governor to treat people with dignity, to be fair even to those who oppose him, and to control his anger. He warns against abusing authority and reminds him not to isolate himself from the public. A leader, he explains, must remain accessible, aware of the struggles of the people, and sensitive to their needs. Within this letter appears one of his most famous sayings, a sentence that captures the heart of his leadership philosophy: "People are of two types: your brothers in faith, or your equals in humanity." With these words, he defined governance as a moral responsibility toward all people, not just one group or faction.

These speeches endure because they speak to questions that never disappear. Every generation asks what justice means, what leadership requires, and what role the material world should play in a human life. Imam Ali's words continue to offer answers because they are grounded in the human condition itself. They do not depend on the politics of his time. They depend on principles that remain constant across centuries.

When he spoke, he did not aim to impress his listeners. He aimed to awaken them. His speeches were not crafted to gain applause. They were meant to guide hearts and correct behavior. That is why they still live today, not as historical artifacts, but as living lessons. Anyone who reads them with sincerity finds guidance, correction, and a deeper understanding of what it means to lead, to serve, and to live with dignity.

More Speeches:

The Voice of Heart & Reason

Imam Ali's speeches are not ordinary sermons. They reflect the human condition, open windows into leadership, and guide the soul. Each speech reveals a different aspect of his character, his courage, restraint, wisdom, humility, and his deep commitment to justice. Through these speeches, readers meet a man who did not separate thought from action. His words carried the same integrity as his life.

One of his most discussed speeches is the Shiqshiqiyya Sermon. In this speech, preserved in *Nahj al-Balāgha*, Imam Ali speaks openly about the political developments after the Prophet's death. He describes how the caliphate moved away from him through circumstances, pressures, and human decisions. He does not turn the speech into a personal attack. Instead, he explains that he chose patience over confrontation to preserve the unity of the community. He recalls how he watched what he considered his right pass from one leader to another, and how he remained silent for the sake of stability. For a modern reader, this sermon demonstrates moral discipline. It shows a leader who believed that preserving social harmony could be more important than claiming personal authority. It teaches that restraint can sometimes carry more strength than open conflict, and that unity can be protected even at personal cost.

Another group of speeches deals with the nature of friendship and brotherhood. In several passages, Imam Ali explains that the best friend is the one who tells the truth, not the one who simply agrees. He warns against surrounding oneself with flatterers and praises the value of honest companionship. His understanding of brotherhood is practical and ethical. Friendship, in his view, is not built on convenience or shared pleasure alone. It is built on character, mutual correction, and sincere concern for one another's growth. For a modern reader, his words remind us that the people we keep close to us shape who we become. He encourages choosing companions who strengthen one's principles rather than those who simply satisfy the ego.

In other sermons, Imam Ali speaks about humility and the dangers of pride. He warns that arrogance blinds the heart and leads to destruction. He reminds his listeners that humility is the natural result of true knowledge. The more a person understands life, the less they are tempted by pride. Ignorance, on the other hand, often produces noise, arrogance, and harshness. This teaching applies to anyone with influence, whether a leader, a teacher, a parent, or a scholar. Imam Ali lived according to this principle. Despite his reputation for courage and knowledge, he dressed simply, lived modestly, and walked among the poor without distance or ceremony. His life gave weight to his words.

Some of his sayings address the condition of the human heart. He observed that hearts grow tired just as bodies do, and he advised people to give them rest through wisdom. He also said that the value of a person lies in what they do well. These words reveal his deep understanding of human psychology. He recognized that people become exhausted not only from work but from confusion, distraction, and lack of meaning. He did not recommend escape through noise or entertainment. He recommended reflection, wisdom, and purposeful action. For him, growth came from recognizing one's strengths and developing them with sincerity.

In another sermon, he speaks about fate and free will. When asked about destiny, he explained that human life is a path between two paths. People are neither forced into every action nor completely independent of divine knowledge. They act, choose, and strive within conditions they did not create. Birth, time, place, and circumstance all shape the possibilities available to them. His explanation offers balance. It encourages people to take responsibility for their choices while accepting what lies beyond their control. This perspective brings discipline to those who neglect responsibility and peace to those who worry about outcomes they cannot control.

These speeches remain relevant because the questions they address never disappear. Every human being faces the tension between truth and falsehood, courage and fear, humility and pride, justice and injustice, hope and despair. Imam Ali's words continue to resonate because they speak directly to these universal struggles. They do not belong to a single community or century. They belong to anyone searching for moral clarity.

His voice has carried across time because it speaks to the

deeper layers of the human soul. It does not rely on slogans or empty emotions. It relies on principles, character, and lived experience. Through these speeches, the reader encounters a historical figure, a guide whose wisdom remains alive in every age.

More Speeches: The Soul in His Words

Imam Ali's speeches were never crafted to impress an audience. They were the natural expression of truth spoken by a man whose heart was aligned with clarity. His words carried a weight that came from the harmony between his character, his conscience, and his actions. When he spoke, he revealed the depth of his insight and the tenderness of his soul. What survives from those speeches is not only eloquence, but guidance that continues to reach readers across centuries.

1. **The Sermon of the Pious (Nahj al-Balāgha, Sermon 193, "Khutbat al-Hammām")**

When asked to describe the qualities of the truly God-conscious, Imam Ali delivered one of the most detailed portraits of spiritual excellence in early Islamic literature. He described the pious as people whose hearts are humble, whose desires are controlled, whose speech is measured, and whose actions are sincere. He portrayed them as patient in hardship, careful in their steps, modest in their gaze, and alive in their hearts. He spoke of people who avoid harming others, forgive quickly, speak truthfully, live lightly in the world, and prepare for the next life with awareness.

Interpretation for Today:

This sermon functions as a reminder for the reader. Imam Ali is not describing unreachable saints. He is describing the qualities that can grow within any person who lives with awareness, restraint, and moral discipline. His words show that spirituality is not withdrawal from life. It is responsibility in the middle of it. Piety is not sadness or isolation. It is self-knowledge, balance, and sincerity.

Humility is not weakness. It is strength governed by conscience. Through this sermon, he sketches the image of a human being who lives with intention, aware of their words, their actions, and their purpose.

2. The Sermon of the Opening Creation (Nahj al-Balāgha, Sermon 1)

In the opening sermon of Nahj al-Balāgha, Imam Ali describes the creation of the universe with powerful language. He speaks of a world formed with balance, purpose, and order. He describes the earth, the heavens, the winds, the mountains, and the stars as part of a creation shaped with intention, not randomness. He emphasizes that God established creation without a prior model and without assistance, a reminder of divine independence and wisdom.

Interpretation for Today:

In this sermon, Imam Ali teaches a foundational perspective about existence. Life is not chaos without meaning. Creation reflects purpose and balance. For the modern reader, surrounded by uncertainty and distraction, these words offer a reminder that existence carries intention. They encourage awareness, gratitude, and humility. The sermon does not present creation as an abstract theory. It presents it as a living reality that calls the human being toward reflection and responsibility.

3. The Sermon of the Silence of the Wise (Nahj al-Balāgha, Saying 147)

Imam Ali said that the wise person remains silent until asked, while the ignorant person keeps speaking until stopped. This short statement reflects his understanding of knowledge, speech, and restraint.

Interpretation for Today:

This teaching is not simply advice about talking less. It is a lesson about the dignity of restraint. Wisdom begins with listening, to others, to experience, to the inner conscience, and to the truth itself. Silence, in Imam Ali's understanding, is not emptiness. It is reflection and preparation. A leader who speaks without thought damages trust. A parent who speaks without listening wounds the child. A teacher who talks without understanding fails the student. His words call for depth in an age often filled with noise and haste.

4. The Sermon of the Eternal Struggle (Nahj al-Balāgha, Sermon 156)

In this sermon, Imam Ali explains that the struggle between truth and falsehood is continuous. He observes that deception often presents itself as honesty, and that injustice sometimes appears attractive. He reminds his listeners that both truth and falsehood have followers, and he urges them to stand among the people of truth.

Interpretation for Today:

Imam Ali is not speaking about armies or political battles. He is speaking about the struggle inside the human heart. Every person carries competing impulses, pride and humility, sincerity and self-interest, courage, and fear. Each day requires choices. His message prepares the reader for reality. The path of truth is not always easy. Falsehood often appears convenient. Still, he offers reassurance. The one who moves toward truth, even slowly, remains on a noble path. The one who moves toward falsehood, even with praise from others, distances himself from his own soul. This sermon reminds readers that goodness requires effort and conscious choice.

5. The Sermon of Leadership as a Burden (Nahj al-Balāgha, Sermon 205)

When Imam Ali accepted the caliphate, he explained that he had not sought it. He said that if people had not insisted, and if he had not felt morally bound to confront oppression and hunger among the people, he would have left the matter alone. He described leadership as a heavy responsibility rather than a personal prize.

Interpretation for Today:

In this sermon, Imam Ali presents leadership as a moral obligation. He did not seek authority for fame or control. He accepted it because injustice needed to be confronted and the vulnerable needed protection. His words challenge modern ideas that treat leadership as an achievement or a reward. He teaches that true leadership is service. It is accepting responsibility because conscience demands it. It is speaking because silence would harm others. It is carrying the burden because the people need someone to carry it.

6. The Sermon on the Nature of Hypocrisy (Nahj al-Balāgha, Sermon 86)

Imam Ali described hypocrisy as a disease of the heart. He warned that hypocrites hide their intentions behind pleasing words, use religion for advantage, and betray trust. He portrayed them as people who speak to deceive and act to harm.

Interpretation for Today:

His insight into hypocrisy is moral and psychological. He defines it as dishonesty of character, saying what one does not mean, presenting virtue while hiding corruption, seeking praise without sincerity, and harming others while pretending kindness. His advice encourages vigilance. People should be judged by their actions, not their claims. Flattery should not replace discernment. The heart should remain sincere even in environments that reward deception. For Imam Ali, hypocrisy is not a minor weakness. It is a slow erosion of the soul.

7. The Sermon of Guidance and Confusion (Nahj al-Balāgha, Sermon 17)

Imam Ali warned that in times of confusion, people often mistake truth for falsehood and falsehood for truth. He advised that individuals should not measure truth. Instead, people should learn the truth first, and then recognize those who follow it.

Interpretation for Today:

This teaching establishes a foundational rule of wisdom. People should not follow personalities without reflection. They should follow principles. Leaders rise and fall. Movements succeed and collapse. Public opinion shifts quickly. Truth remains the only stable guide. In a world of misinformation, emotional rhetoric, and constant persuasion, his words offer a steady reference point. They remind readers to anchor themselves to ethical and moral principles. When a person is grounded in truth, they know where they stand, regardless of who is popular or powerful.

These speeches reveal something essential about Imam Ali. He was not only a warrior, a leader, or a wise scholar. He was a man whose heart saw with clarity and wished for others to see with the same clarity. His speeches are not relics of a distant past. They are living lessons that speak to the struggles of every person, the challenges of every age, and the responsibilities carried by anyone entrusted with influence. Imam Ali spoke to his own time, but his wisdom belongs to all time.

His Letters:

Leadership Written with a Heart

History remembers Imam Ali as a warrior, a wise scholar, a philosopher, a judge, and a leader. But to understand the depth of his character, one must read his letters. They offer perhaps the clearest view into his inner life, written not for ceremony or applause, but for governors who needed guidance, commanders who required discipline, and a son who needed a father's wisdom. In these letters, his voice is direct, sincere, and deeply human.

They were preserved not because they belonged to an empire, but because they carried the moral weight of a man who refused to separate authority from conscience. Through them, we see a form of leadership that does not rely on fear, spectacle, or strategy alone. Instead, it rests on dignity, fairness, and a steady awareness of human suffering.

The Letter to His Governor Malik al-Ashtar

When Imam Ali appointed Malik al-Ashtar to govern Egypt, he did not praise him with titles or prepare him with political tactics. He handed him a letter that reads more like a moral covenant than an administrative order. Imam Ali understood how power can reshape a person. He knew leadership could test even the most sincere soul. So he began not with laws or systems, but with the heart.

He instructed Malik to treat every person under his authority with dignity. The people, he wrote, were not subjects to be managed but human beings with fears, hopes, and needs. He warned him that authority can intoxicate, that pride quietly enters the heart of a ruler, and that justice requires gentleness as much as strength.

Imam Ali spoke to Malik in the tone of a father guiding a son. He told him to protect the poor before the wealthy, to speak with kindness even in moments of anger, and to govern in a way that allowed both the oppressed and the powerful to sleep without fear. He urged him to walk among the people rather than hide behind guards, to listen before commanding, and to remember that every citizen is either a brother in faith or an equal in humanity.

In those words, Imam Ali drew one of the earliest and clearest models of humane leadership. Long before formal constitutions or charters of rights, he wrote a letter that still stands as a guide for anyone entrusted with authority.

The Letter to Uthman ibn Hunayf

Another letter reveals a different dimension of his character, the side of him that could not accept social inequality without response. When his governor in Basra attended a banquet where the wealthy gathered while the poor were absent, Imam Ali wrote to him with firm and measured words.

He reminded him that leadership is not companionship with the privileged. It is solidarity with those who struggle. A leader who sits at a table closed to the poor, he warned, has already forgotten his purpose. He described his own simple clothing and coarse bread, not to display virtue, but to remind his governor that a ruler must remain aware of the condition of the people.

He explained that he could easily choose fine food and comfortable living if he wished, but how could he feel satisfied while others around him lacked even a simple meal. These words did not come from a palace or a throne. They came from a conscience shaped by empathy and restraint.

He was not calling for misery. He was calling for awareness. Not demanding hardship, but humility. He wanted his governors to feel the pulse of the society they served.

The Letter to His Son Hasan

Among his letters, the one addressed to his son Hasan stands apart for its tenderness and depth. It is not the voice of a ruler or judge. It is the voice of a father who has lived through conflict, loss, and responsibility, and who wishes to spare his child unnecessary pain.

He begins by telling Hasan that he sees him not simply as a son, but as a part of his own being. He writes because he has witnessed the fragility of life and the deceptions of the world. He wants his son to move through life with awareness, not illusion.

He advises him to guard his heart from arrogance, to keep the company of the righteous, and to stand beside the oppressed. He explains that the heart of youth is fertile ground, and whatever is planted there will shape the rest of a person's life.

He encourages balance, telling him to work for this world with diligence, while preparing for the next with sincerity.

The letter offers a philosophy of time, character, and responsibility. It is not only advice from a father to a son. It is guidance for every person who seeks direction, and for every parent who hopes to raise a child with integrity.

The Power of His Letters

Together, these letters present a portrait of Imam Ali that cannot be seen in battles or public speeches alone. In them, we encounter the tenderness of a father, the precision of a judge, the empathy of a defender of the weak, the humility of a servant, and the clarity of a man who saw leadership as a moral trust.

They show a leader who did not hide behind his authority, who expected justice even when it was inconvenient, and who spoke to governors with the same honesty he used with his own children. His letters do not feel like relics from a distant era. They read like living documents of conscience, written by a man whose moral clarity still speaks to the modern world.

Imam Ali did not write for the sake of reputation or historical record. He wrote to guide human beings. That is why his letters continue to live, not only in books, but in the hearts of those who seek to lead with integrity, to live with purpose, and to rise above the temptations of power.

His Prayers: When a Noble Heart Speaks to God

There are moments in a person's life when words rise not from the tongue but from the depths of the soul. In those moments, language changes. It softens, it becomes lighter, more honest, stripped of pride and free from performance. For Imam Ali, prayer was not a ritual to complete or a duty to fulfill, it was the place where the warrior laid down his armor, the leader lowered his voice, and the judge sought guidance from the One who needs no counselor. His prayers preserved through history reveal a man whose strength came not from power but from surrender, not from certainty but from humility.

When Imam Ali prayed, he did not pretend to be fearless, although he was the bravest of men. He did not pretend to be sinless, though his character was unmatched. He did not come before God boasting of victories or sacrifices. Instead, he came as a servant who knew the fragility of the human soul, the weight of leadership, and the limits of human understanding. His prayers carry a tone of sincerity that cannot be imitated; they contain a softness that stands in contrast to the fierceness of the battlefield and the thunder of his sermons.

One of the most cherished prayers attributed to him is the whispered supplication known as *Duʿāʾ Kumayl*, taught to his companion Kumayl ibn Ziyād. It is not a political document, nor a legal ruling, nor a moral instruction. It is Imam Ali's heart speaking to God with the intimacy of one who knows that every breath is a gift and every mistake a reminder of human imperfection. In it, he admits weakness and pleads for mercy, not because he sees himself as unworthy, but because he sees God as infinitely generous. He speaks of his remorse, his hope, his fear, and his longing, revealing a soul fully awake to its dependence on divine compassion.

There is a profound honesty in the way Imam Ali prays. He does not exaggerate his piety or hide his vulnerability. He confesses the smallness of human beings before the vastness of the Creator. In his words, one feels both the tremor of awe and the comfort of closeness. He speaks of God as the One who forgives more than we deserve, who gives more than we ask, and who responds to the call of the broken-hearted even when they feel unworthy. Through his prayers, Imam Ali teaches that strength is not the absence of fear but the ability to bring that fear to God with trust.

There is another prayer in which Imam Ali describes the restlessness of the human heart. He speaks of desires that mislead, doubts that cloud judgment, and burdens that become too heavy to carry alone. Yet he ends the supplication not in despair but in quiet confidence, trusting that God's mercy is wider than human shortcomings. His prayers often begin with humility and end with hope, reminding the reader that the journey to God is not a path for the perfect but for those who are honest with themselves.

In these intimate words, we see a truth that his battles and leadership cannot show. Imam Ali was not only a man of action but a man of reflection. He understood both the public demands of leadership and the private needs of the soul. He knew that no matter how wise, brave, or just a person becomes, the heart can lose its way without constant grounding in prayer. For him, prayer was not an escape from responsibility, but the source of the strength needed to shoulder it.

The tenderness found in his supplications contrasts with the image of the fearless warrior who never retreated in battle. In prayer, he reveals that courage comes not from the absence of fear but from the presence of God. It comes from recognizing one's limits and turning inward to the One who has none. It is in this softness, this vulnerability, this whispered humility that the reader finds the deepest layers of Imam Ali's character. The man who stood unshaken before armies stood humbled before God.

What makes these prayers timeless is not their poetry, though their poetry is unmatched, but their humanity. Every person, regardless of faith or background, can hear themselves in his words: the struggle to do right, the grief of failure, the longing for forgiveness, the desire for clarity, the need for strength, the search for peace. Imam Ali speaks with the voice of someone who has lived through joy and anguish, victory and loss, loyalty, and betrayal. His supplications hold the wisdom of a man who carried both the sword of justice and the weight of human sorrow.

In the end, his prayers teach us that greatness is never separate from humility, that leadership is never separate from dependence on God, and that the noblest hearts are those that speak to the heavens with honesty. Imam Ali prayed the way he lived, with sincerity, courage, and a deep awareness of the fragility and beauty of the human soul.

His judgments:
Justice in the Hands of a Noble Heart

The true measure of a leader is revealed when he sits not on a horse in battle, but on the judge's seat with two people standing before him, each claiming to be right. It is in these moments that the world sees the nature of a man's heart, whether it bends with power or remains straight with truth. Imam Ali's judgments became legendary not because they were clever, but because they were rooted in a soul incapable of injustice. He judged the way he lived, calmly, fairly, and with a conscience that refused to bow to fear, favor, or emotion.

One of the most famous cases occurred when Imam Ali, while serving as Caliph, lost a shield he had used in battle. Later, he found it with a Christian man in Kufa. Rather than reclaim it by authority, he took the man to court, insisting they stand as equals before the judge, Shurayh al-Qadi. The judge asked Imam Ali for evidence that the shield was his. Imam Ali smiled gently; he had no witnesses. Shurayh ruled in favor of the Christian man, and Imam Ali accepted the verdict without argument.

The Christian man, stunned by the fairness of a ruler who did not use his position to win a case, confessed that the shield indeed belonged to Imam Ali. He embraced Islam not because he was forced or persuaded, but because he saw justice that felt divine. This case became a symbol of the dignity Imam Ali extended to non-Muslims and of the moral discipline with which he held himself accountable.

In another case, two women came before him, each claiming to be the mother of the same infant. There were no witnesses, no documents, and no way to determine who was telling the truth. Imam Ali watched the women carefully, not with suspicion but with the attentiveness of someone who understood human emotion. He asked for a blade. Shocked, the women looked at him. Imam Ali said he would divide the child in half so each woman would receive an equal portion. One woman remained silent. The other cried out, begging him not to harm the child, even if it meant losing him. Imam Ali immediately handed the infant to her. He knew the true mother is the one who prefers pain over seeing her child harmed. His judgment was not only correct, it was compassionate. He saw truth through a mother's heart.

There was another moment, quieter but just as revealing, when a man came to complain that a governor had treated him unjustly. Imam Ali did not dismiss him nor favor his governor. He summoned the governor into the room and insisted that the man sit as an equal beside him. The governor hesitated, embarrassed to sit beside an ordinary person. Imam Ali corrected him firmly, reminding him that no one sits above another when seeking justice. He then warned the governor that injustice from a leader is a betrayal of God's trust. His voice was calm, but the room felt the weight of his words. His justice did not rise only in court; it lived in the way he taught rulers to see themselves.

In yet another case, a woman accused a man of wrongdoing, and Imam Ali instructed that she be treated with full respect while the matter was investigated. When the man mocked the accusation, Imam Ali reminded him that truth does not depend on gender, wealth, or status. He insisted that voices often dismissed by society must be heard with fairness. He once said that justice is the balance by which the world survives. His judgments embodied that balance, lifting the weak without humiliating the strong and correcting the strong without crushing their dignity.

There were times Imam Ali judged in ways that revealed not only intelligence but moral courage. When two men came before him, one wealthy and one poor, he noticed the wealthy man instinctively stepping closer to him. Imam Ali warned him immediately, telling him not to stand in a way that might intimidate his opponent. Then he turned to the poor man and told him not to let poverty weaken his confidence, for justice sees hearts, not wealth. In that moment, he was not simply delivering a verdict; he was teaching both men about equality before God.

Imam Ali's judgments were not clever tricks or theatrical displays. They were the natural result of a soul that could not tolerate oppression in any form. He believed that justice is the breath of society and that a single unjust ruling could corrupt an entire community. He used the courtroom not as a place to display authority, but as a sanctuary where truth could stand upright again.

He once said that the weak should never despair of justice and the strong should never feel above it. The sincerity of these words lived in every decision he made. People trusted him not because he was caliph, but because he was incapable of bending truth for anyone, including himself.

What made Imam Ali's judgments unforgettable was not the brilliance of his mind, though he possessed a mind sharper than the finest sword. What made them unforgettable was the purity of his heart. His justice was an extension of who he was, a man who feared God, loved humanity, and believed that fairness is the highest form of worship.

A society led by Imam Ali tasted what justice feels like when it is delivered by a heart that refuses to compromise. His judgments are not historical episodes; they are lessons that still instruct the world. They remind leaders what leadership truly means, remind judges what fairness requires, and remind ordinary people that justice, when practiced with sincerity, can illuminate the darkest corridors of society.

The Noble Heart of Humanity

To understand Imam Ali's life, one must first understand how he saw the world. His philosophy was not a collection of theories or abstractions. It was the quiet logic of a man who lived with courage, led with humility, and prayed with sincerity. His understanding of life came from experience, from standing at the Prophet's side, from governing a nation torn by politics, from raising children with tenderness, from battling oppression, and from wrestling with his own soul in the darkness of the night.

Imam Ali believed that life is a journey of the heart as much as it is a journey of the body. He saw the human being as a creature pulled between two forces: the pull of ego and the call of conscience. Every decision, every reaction, every temptation, every act of kindness reveals which of these two holds the reins. For him, the purpose of life was not to escape hardship but to refine the soul through it. He once said that a person is tested not by comfort but by challenge, and that strength is born in the moments when one chooses restraint over impulse.

He saw the world with startling clarity. Its beauty did not deceive him, and its ugliness did not discourage him. He understood that everything temporary is designed to teach a lesson, not to grant permanence. When he spoke of the dunya (life), he did not condemn it with bitterness or exaggeration.

He simply reminded people that the world is a place of

passing shadows, useful, necessary, beautiful in parts, but never to be mistaken for a final home. What harms a person is not the world itself, but the illusion that the world is everything.

Imam Ali believed that the true measure of a person lies not in wealth, lineage, or status, but in character. He valued knowledge above possessions and sincerity above praise. He once said that the worth of any human being is what they do well, meaning that a person's value is not in what they claim, but in the actions they consistently live. He believed that intention is the seed of every action and that even the smallest deed becomes great when done with pure motives.

He taught that the mind is a trust, the heart a sanctuary, and the body a vehicle. To him, wisdom was not to be stored but practiced. A wise person is not the one with the most information but the one who sees clearly, acts justly, and speaks truthfully. He valued contemplation as much as action, believing that silence can sometimes teach more than speech. He understood the human tendency to rush, to react, to judge prematurely, and he reminded people that patience is a companion of wisdom.

His philosophy of life rested on the concept of balance, a balance between courage and caution, ambition and humility, justice and mercy, this world and the next. He did not promote excess in anything. He believed that moderation protects the soul from corruption and the heart from being overwhelmed. Even in worship, he warned against extremism, saying that the heart grows tired and must be guided gently, never forced, or broken.

Above all, Imam Ali believed that the human heart is the ruler of a person's destiny. If the heart is clear, life becomes clear. If the heart is darkened by pride, greed, or arrogance, the path becomes foggy no matter how intelligent or wealthy a person may be. He saw arrogance as the first sign of downfall, because it blinds the mind to truth and closes the heart to compassion. To him, humility was not weakness but a form of inner strength, the ability to see oneself honestly without exaggeration or denial.

He believed that truth is a light that does not dim, even when people turn away from it. Falsehood, no matter how glamorous, eventually collapses. His life proved this. He saw leaders rise through deceit and fall through the weight of their own lies. He saw communities shaken by rumors and steadied by truth. And he taught that a person should always walk toward truth, even if the path is steep and lonely, because truth is the only companion that never betrays.

Imam Ali taught that forgiveness is not merely an act of mercy but an act of liberation, freeing oneself from the burden of anger. He knew that holding onto resentment imprisons the heart, and that forgiveness releases it back into clarity. He forgave enemies not because he was weak, but because he refused to let hatred dictate the condition of his soul.

His philosophy can be condensed into one simple idea: Live with a heart that remembers God, a mind that seeks wisdom, and a character that harms no one.

In a world that constantly pulls the human being toward greed, pride, and distraction, Imam Ali's teachings remain a guide toward balance, dignity, and purpose. He saw life not as a race but as a trust, a trust to be honored, a journey to be lived with awareness, and an opportunity to refine the soul before returning to the One who created it.

His philosophy does not belong to a single religion or a single era. It belongs to every human being who wishes to rise above the noise of the world and live with clarity, humility, and truth.

His Moral Code: The Inner Compass of a Noble Soul

Every great figure in history is remembered for what they did. Imam Ali is remembered for why he did it. His legacy does not rest only in the battles he fought or the speeches he delivered, but in the moral code that shaped every decision he made. It was a moral code not built from circumstance, but formed in the home of the Prophet, shaped by the presence of revelation, and refined by the purity of his own heart. His actions did not rise from strategy. They rose from principle.

Imam Ali lived with an inner clarity that made right and wrong unmistakable. He never chased reputation, nor did he fear criticism. For him, morality was not a mask worn in public. It was a commitment to truth, no matter how uncomfortable or costly. He believed that when a person compromises their values, even once, the soul begins a slow erosion. His life demonstrated that principles must be lived consistently, especially when they challenge one's desires or pride.

At the center of his moral code stood honesty, a fierce and unshakable honesty that refused to bend. He taught that truth does not change because people dislike it, and falsehood does not become right because people applaud it. This belief guided his leadership. He never hid behind diplomacy to excuse injustice, and he never softened truth to gain allies. He spoke with sincerity that sometimes made people uneasy, but it also made him incomparable. His honesty was not harsh or cruel. It was steady, calm, and grounded in a conscience he would never betray.

Humility formed another pillar of his character. Despite being the most knowledgeable companion of the Prophet, the bravest soldier in early Islam, and the rightful heir to leadership, Imam Ali never behaved as if he were above others. He walked among the poor with ease, carried food to widows in the night, and lived in a simple home even when he governed a vast land. He taught that arrogance is a veil that prevents a person from seeing themselves clearly. His humility was not an act. It was the natural dignity of someone who understood that every breath is a gift.

His moral code also demanded generosity, not only with wealth, but with time, effort, and compassion. He believed that kindness is a form of worship, and that a gentle word, a lifted burden, or a forgiven mistake carries great weight with God. He gave even when he had little, served even when he was tired, and forgave even when he had been wronged. His generosity was never a performance. It was simply the way he moved through life.

Justice stood as a central point of his moral compass. Imam Ali never allowed personal relationships to shape his decisions. His own brother, Aqeel, once asked him for extra money from the public treasury. Imam Ali heated a small piece of metal and brought it close to Aqeel's hand, asking how he could request something that belonged to the people. Aqeel recoiled in pain, and Imam Ali reminded him that if he could not withstand a small heat, how could he expect his brother to endure the fire of divine judgment for betraying the trust of the community. His justice did not favor family over strangers, or friends over opponents. It favored truth alone.

Mercy also lived deep within his moral code. He believed that the heart grows stronger when it forgives. On the battlefield, where cruelty is often expected, Imam Ali refused to allow hatred to rule him. He never pursued a wounded enemy, never mocked an opponent, and never allowed humiliation or gloating. On one occasion, when he defeated a warrior and the man fell unarmed before him, Imam Ali stepped back rather than strike. The warrior, moved by this restraint, later accepted Islam through admiration rather than force. Imam Ali showed that mercy is not the opposite of strength. It is the proof of it.

Self-control formed another essential part of his character. He believed that a person who cannot govern their own impulses has no right to govern others. Anger, in his view, was the enemy of wisdom. He once told his son Hasan that anger begins with madness and ends in regret. Imam Ali never allowed rage to cloud his judgment, and he never allowed ambition to harden his heart.

At its essence, his moral code was a life lived with awareness: awareness of God, awareness of responsibility, awareness of people's needs, and awareness of one's own faults. He believed accountability begins within the self, and that no leader can guide others without first guiding their own heart.

He taught that a noble life is not measured by victories, but by integrity; not by status, but by sincerity; not by wealth, but by the purity of intention. His moral code was not a list of rules. It was a way of being, a way that appeared in every word he spoke, every judgment he made, every battle he entered, and every prayer he whispered in the stillness of the night.

In the end, the greatness of Imam Ali rests not only in what he accomplished, but in how he lived. His moral code was the lamp that lit his path, and it remains a lamp for anyone who wishes to walk through life with dignity, clarity, and a heart anchored in truth.

His Influence Across Civilizations

The life of Imam Ali did not end with his martyrdom. It began to travel. It crossed deserts and mountains, moved through languages and cultures, and found its way into books, institutions, philosophies, and hearts. His influence did not remain within the early Islamic world. It moved beyond the borders of Arabia and beyond his own era, reaching people who had never heard of the battles he fought or the sermons he delivered. His life became a mirror in which different civilizations recognized qualities they admired but rarely found united in one person, courage and compassion, power and humility, wisdom and action, spirituality, and justice.

In the centuries that followed, scholars from diverse backgrounds wrote about him with admiration. Historians in Europe recorded him as a model of chivalry. Poets in Persia described him as the sword of truth. Philosophers in India and the Levant saw in him a teacher of ethics. Spiritual seekers across continents recognized in his voice a purity they longed for. His name became a symbol of justice wherever people suffered under oppression.

In the medieval world, some Christian chroniclers who studied Islamic history paused at his character and described him as a man whose loyalty knew no compromise and whose bravery had no equal. They were struck by a personality so gentle with the weak and so fearless in battle, so devoted to

God and so present among people, so principled that even his enemies recorded his virtues. In their writings, Imam Ali appeared as the embodiment of the ideal knight, a defender of truth who lived with honor untouched by power.

In Persia, poets and thinkers saw in him the union of intellect and spirituality. His sayings about the soul, time, patience, knowledge, and the human condition inspired verses that still echo in Persian literature. Writers such as Rumi, Saadi, and Hafez drew from his wisdom, sometimes directly and sometimes through the ethical world he helped shape. For them, he represented the human being who walks with God without abandoning humanity, the one who carries a sword in defense of justice while keeping mercy close to the heart.

In South Asia, his sense of justice influenced legal and ethical discussions across many schools of thought. Scholars studied his judgments as examples of how law and compassion can coexist, how principles can guide decisions without losing sight of the individual. His letter to Malik al-Ashtar was translated into several languages and admired as a political document known for its fairness and concern for human dignity, long before modern language of human rights became common.

Even thinkers who did not share his faith were drawn to his clarity of thought. They found in his words a balance between intellect and spirituality that few historical figures possess. In his teachings, they discovered that knowledge without humility becomes arrogance, that power without justice becomes oppression, and that leadership without conscience becomes tyranny.

His influence also spread through the world of spirituality beyond formal religious boundaries. Sufi teachers across many regions looked to him as a gateway of inner knowledge. They saw in him the balance of discipline and compassion, action and reflection, outward strength, and inward surrender. For them, Imam Ali was not simply a figure of history. He was a model of spiritual maturity, someone who understood the struggles of the soul and the path toward purification.

Perhaps the greatest measure of Imam Ali's influence is not found in books, poetry, or intellectual debates. It is found in the human longing for a leader like him. People across cultures, even those who do not know his name, search for the qualities he embodied: justice without cruelty, strength without arrogance, intelligence without manipulation, simplicity without weakness, spirituality without escape from responsibility. His life answers a universal question about what it means for a human being to rise above ego and live with integrity in every situation.

Civilizations have risen and fallen since his time, but Imam Ali remains a point of reference because he represents a possibility, the possibility of leadership guided by conscience, of faith grounded in sincerity, of courage that protects rather than destroys, of wisdom that unites rather than divides. He stands as proof that greatness is not measured by power alone but by the intention behind it.

His influence continues because he lived the values that civilizations admire but struggle to practice. Justice, humility, courage, wisdom, compassion, he carried them all in balance. His legacy did not fade with empires or dynasties. It moved quietly through hearts, minds, and generations, becoming timeless.

Imam Ali belongs not only to the history of Islam but to the history of humanity. His life reminds us that moral greatness does not age, true wisdom does not lose relevance, and a noble heart continues to illuminate every place it reaches.

His Teachings for Modern Leadership

Leadership today is more complex than any era before it. Nations rise and fall under the weight of decisions made by those in power. Companies flourish or collapse because of the character of the people at the top. Families, communities, and institutions succeed or fail depending on whether leaders serve their people or serve themselves. In a world overwhelmed by ambition, ego, competition, and noise, the teachings of Imam Ali enter like a calm, steady light, timeless, clear, and relevant.

Modern leaders search for frameworks, strategies, and systems. Imam Ali offered something deeper, a way of being. He taught that leadership begins with the heart, not the office, with character, not credentials. He understood that authority without integrity becomes corruption, and ambition without conscience becomes destruction. His guidance was not written for one time or one place. It was written for leaders in every generation, including those navigating today's crowded and complicated world.

One of his first lessons for modern leadership is the reminder that power is a trust, not a throne. He believed that a leader's authority exists only to uplift, protect, and guide. He wrote that God has made the strong responsible for the weak, and that leaders are held accountable for every injustice committed under their watch. In an era where many pursue influence for personal gain, his voice calls leadership back to accountability, the kind that cannot be hidden behind excuses or polished appearances.

Another essential teaching is his insistence that justice must be the foundation of all governance. For Imam Ali, justice was not an intellectual concept. It was a living commitment. He never allowed favoritism, even toward those he loved most. No modern leader can study his actions without feeling challenged. In a world where corruption often hides behind charm and alliances, he shows what it means to stand firm. He teaches that a leader who bends justice once for convenience begins a slow decay of their own authority.

His approach to humility offers a model needed in every age. Modern leadership often rewards visibility and ego, the louder voice, the bigger presence, the illusion of invincibility. Imam Ali lived differently. He walked in markets without guards, carried food to the poor at night, and refused luxuries even when they were available to him. He reminded leaders that humility is not weakness but clarity, the clarity to see the people you serve rather than the position you hold.

He also taught the importance of listening, truly listening, not as performance but as a responsibility. He believed that leaders must walk among their people, hear their needs directly, and never isolate themselves behind privilege or authority. Today, leaders are often separated by screens, schedules, and status. Imam Ali's example closes that distance and reminds us that separation creates distrust, and distrust weakens leadership from within.

Courage, for Imam Ali, was not recklessness but moral clarity. Many leaders confuse boldness with arrogance, or flexibility with weakness. He showed that courage is the ability to stand firmly on truth even when alone, and humility is the ability to step back when wrong. He lived both qualities with ease. He never compromised his values to gain an ally, and he forgave an enemy when compassion was the better path. His courage was not theatrical. It was principled.

Integrity defined every choice he made. He taught that the private life of a leader is as important as the public one. Many try to separate the two. Imam Ali did not. He believed the heart that lies in private will eventually betray its surroundings in public. The person who cheats quietly will one day cheat openly. For him, leadership required inner discipline, truthfulness, and sincerity at all hours, not only when others were watching.

Another timeless teaching is his approach to anger. He believed that anger is the fastest path to injustice and the slowest path to wisdom. Leaders under pressure often react and make decisions clouded by emotion. Imam Ali reminded them that patience is not passivity. It is precision. It is the discipline that keeps judgment clear when emotions try to take control.

He also believed that leaders should nurture the strengths of their people. He taught that the worth of every human being lies in what they excel at. In a world where many leaders compete with their teams or fear talented individuals, Imam Ali teaches that true leaders lift others higher. Their success becomes the leader's success, and their growth becomes a sign of the leader's wisdom.

Finally, he taught that leadership must be tied to purpose. Without purpose, power becomes empty. Without values, authority becomes dangerous. For him, the purpose of leadership was to protect, to guide, and to bring justice to every corner of society. Leaders search for visions and missions. Imam Ali reminds them that the highest mission is to serve humanity with fairness, humility, and courage.

His teachings remain alive because they speak directly to the inner life of a leader, not the public image but the internal truth. They offer guidance for presidents and parents, CEOs and teachers, commanders, and community organizers. They show that the most effective leadership is not loud but steady, not forceful but principled, not arrogant but wise.

In a world hungry for integrity, Imam Ali remains an example. In a world confused about power, he remains a compass. In a world weighed down by moral fatigue, he remains a reminder of what leadership can look like when guided by a noble heart.

His View of Human Character

Imam Ali understood human beings with a clarity that feels almost impossible. He saw beyond the outer layers, beyond status, reputation, or behavior, into the inner forces that shape a person's choices. He understood that every human being carries within them a battlefield: desires that pull, conscience that whispers, fears that distort, hopes that inspire. His view of character was not judgmental but compassionate. He did not expect perfection; he expected honesty. He believed that a person's greatness lies not in always being right but in always returning to what is right.

To Imam Ali, the human being is a creature of intention. Actions matter, but intentions reveal the heart. He often taught that the value of an action is determined by the sincerity behind it. A small deed done with a pure heart becomes great, while a large deed done for show becomes empty. He understood how the ego disguises itself, how people may claim virtue while chasing approval, or appear strong while hiding insecurity. He taught that the first step toward good character is truthfulness with oneself.

He believed that the heart is the leader of the body. If the heart is pure, the limbs follow in goodness; if the heart is corrupted, no outward performance can mask it. He did not judge people by moments of weakness, for he knew that weakness is part of the human design. But he warned that habits shape destiny. What a person does repeatedly becomes who they are. A small dishonesty repeated becomes character;

a small kindness repeated becomes character. For Imam Ali, character was not built in grand moments but in the consistent choices made every day.

He saw pride as the greatest threat to human character. He believed arrogance blinds the mind, hardens the heart, and isolates a person from truth. Pride prevents growth because it convinces a person they have already arrived. He taught that humility is not self-denial but self-awareness, the ability to see one's strengths without denying one's flaws. Humility allows a person to learn, to apologize, to reflect, and to change. For him, humility was the foundation of wisdom.

He understood that fear shapes people more than they admit. Some cling to comfort because they fear failure. Others cling to status because they fear insignificance. Some lash out in anger because they fear vulnerability. Imam Ali saw fear not as a moral failure but as a human condition that must be managed with faith, patience, and clarity. He taught that courage is not the absence of fear but the ability to act correctly despite it.

He believed deeply in the power of patience. For him, patience was not passive endurance but active strength. It was the ability to remain steady when faced with hardship, to remain kind when provoked, to remain truthful when pressured. He taught that patience is essential to faith, and that many people fail not because they are incapable but because they abandon their path too soon. Character, in his understanding, is proven not in easy days but in the storms that test the heart.

Imam Ali also saw that envy corrodes the soul. He believed that envy blinds a person to their blessings, distracts them from their potential, and poisons relationships. He taught that a content heart is a peaceful heart and that a peaceful heart becomes a source of goodness for others. Contentment, in his view, was not settling for less but recognizing that inner richness matters more than outer achievements.

He had a profound awareness of how words shape character. He taught that the tongue can elevate a person or ruin them. Words reveal intentions, expose weaknesses, and declare values. He urged people to speak only when their words improve silence. To him, wisdom often lived in restraint.

Imam Ali believed that companionship shapes character more than people realize. He taught that a person is known by the company they keep because the heart absorbs the habits of those around it. He advised people to seek companions who remind them of virtue, who push them toward goodness, and who correct them gently when they stray. He warned against surrounding oneself with those who flatter, exploit, or mislead, for such company damages the soul.

He saw kindness as the most powerful expression of noble character. Kindness for him was not softness but strength, the strength to care, to forgive, to help, and to listen. He believed that every human being carries a burden, and that a person of good character tries to lighten the burdens of others, even in small ways. He understood that character is not measured by how one treats those above them, but by how one treats those with no power at all.

Finally, Imam Ali believed that self-reflection is the engine of character growth. He urged people to examine their motives, actions, and intentions regularly. He taught that the person who holds themselves accountable in private avoids disgrace in public. For him, the greatest victory was not in defeating others but in conquering the weaknesses of one's own soul.

Imam Ali's view of human character is among the most complete ever recorded, realistic yet hopeful, deep yet accessible, firm yet compassionate. He understood that people are flawed but capable of greatness, weak but capable of strength, confused yet capable of clarity. His teachings remind every reader that character is a lifelong journey, and that within every heart there is a path toward nobility waiting to be walked.

His Teachings for the Ordinary Person

Few people will rule a country, lead an army, or deliver sermons and letters that shape civilizations. But everyone will wake up in the morning, face choices, meet people, fight temptations, carry burdens, seek happiness, and search for meaning. Imam Ali understood this better than most. He knew that the majority of humanity lives simple, steady lives, raising children, earning a living, staying hopeful, trying to remain decent even when the world feels harsh. He did not speak only to governors or warriors. He spoke to the heart of the ordinary person, the one who simply wants to live well, die with dignity, and leave behind a life that mattered.

For Imam Ali, living a good life begins with honesty, not the loud honesty that exposes others, but the silent honesty one practices with oneself. He believed that a person must recognize their own weaknesses and intentions before they can improve. He taught that self-deception is the root of many sorrows. The person who lies to themselves walks blindly, even if everyone else sees the truth. He encouraged people to pause, to reflect, to question the impulses that drive them. In this reflection, a person discovers their truest self.

He also believed that a good life requires balance. Too much fear keeps a person from moving forward; too much hope blinds them to danger. Too much work exhausts the soul; too much leisure weakens it. Too much attachment to the world causes disappointment; too much detachment drains joy.

Imam Ali taught people to walk the middle path, steady, thoughtful, and aware. He believed that life was created with purpose and gratitude, not as a burden to escape or a game to waste.

In daily interactions, Imam Ali urged people to treat one another with kindness. He knew that every person carries a silent struggle. A gentle word can lift a heart; a harsh word can break it. He taught that kindness is the least expensive gift but the richest in return. He reminded people that the tongue is small, yet it can build bridges or destroy them. He once said that a person is hidden under their words; only when they speak does their character appear. So he encouraged people to speak with intention, to listen more than they talk, and to choose words that heal rather than wound.

He believed that relationships are among life's greatest tests. He advised people to surround themselves with companions who inspire goodness, honesty, and growth. He warned against keeping company with those who thrive on gossip, arrogance, or manipulation. For Imam Ali, friendship was not entertainment, it was nourishment. A true friend strengthens your character. A false friend weakens it. He taught people to be loyal, to forgive, to correct gently, and to step away from relationships that darken the heart.

Imam Ali also taught that a good life must include service. He believed that helping others lifts the helper before it lifts the one being helped. He lived this truth quietly, feeding widows at night, supporting orphans, and settling disputes without seeking praise. He taught that even a small act of goodness can change the course of a day, or even a life. A person should not wait for perfect circumstances to do good. Goodness should become a habit.

He understood the frustrations of daily living, financial stress, conflicts, disappointments, and losses. He urged people to meet these challenges with patience, not because patience removes pain, but because it protects the heart from breaking under it. He taught that patience is strength, the strength to keep the heart steady when the world shifts around it. He believed that God sees every tear, every effort, every quiet endurance. Nothing is wasted.

A central teaching of Imam Ali is that one should seek knowledge throughout life. Not only the knowledge found in books, but the knowledge of the heart, the knowledge of people, and the knowledge of one's own limitations. He believed that ignorance is the root of many hardships. A person who does not understand themselves cannot understand others. A person who refuses to learn from mistakes repeats them.

He encouraged people to be grateful, not through grand speeches, but through the quiet recognition of blessings that often go unnoticed: health, breath, safety, the ability to walk, the presence of a loved one, a warm meal, a peaceful night. Gratitude, he taught, expands the heart. It turns scarcity into sufficiency, and sufficiency into richness.

He taught people to avoid envy, for envy is a fire that burns only the one who holds it. Instead, he encouraged contentment, not the kind that kills ambition, but the kind that protects the heart from bitterness. He believed that what is meant for a person will reach them, and what is not meant for them cannot be forced into their hands.

Above all, Imam Ali believed that a good life is built on intention, kindness, humility, and awareness. He believed that the ordinary person who lives with sincerity and compassion is more honored in the sight of God than the powerful person who lives only for themselves. He raised the dignity of everyday life and taught that greatness is not measured by status, but by the condition of the heart.

In the end, his teachings remind us that the good life is not complicated. It is a life lived with a clean heart, a sincere tongue, a thoughtful mind, and a gentle presence. He believed that every person, no matter how simple their life may seem, carries the capacity for nobility. And he taught that the path to that nobility is always open.

His Teachings on Family Life

For all his courage on the battlefield and all his brilliance in leadership, Imam Ali's greatness appeared most gently inside his home. It was there, away from armies and politics, that his character revealed its most tender truths. For him, family was not a private obligation but a sacred trust, and the home was the first school where love teaches, character forms, and souls grow.

Imam Ali believed that marriage was not merely a contract but a companionship of hearts. He treated his wife, Fatimah, the daughter of the Prophet, with a tenderness that history still remembers with admiration. Their home was simple, their possessions were few, and still it was filled with affection, courtesy, and mutual respect. He shared the work of the household, carried water, cleaned, and never considered domestic tasks beneath him. He saw partnership not as a division of labor but as a unity of purpose. He understood that love does not live in grand gestures alone, but in the small acts of care repeated every day.

He taught that a spouse is both a mirror and a shelter, someone through whom one improves and in whom one finds peace. He believed that spouses should protect each other's dignity, forgive each other's faults, and support each other's growth.

He reminded people to guard their words inside the home, because the wounds caused by loved ones often cut deeper than those caused by strangers. His marriage showed that love grows strongest when nourished with kindness, patience, and humility.

As a father, Imam Ali's love was vast and gentle. He did not raise his children through fear or harshness, but through presence, wisdom, and example. He believed that children learn more from what a parent lives than from what a parent says. His famous letter to his son Hasan remains one of the most beautiful guides on raising a child, revealing a heart full of compassion and insight. He wrote to him as a friend, a mentor, and a guardian of his future, advising him about the world's temptations, the value of good company, the importance of humility, and the necessity of truthfulness.

He instructed parents to speak to their children according to their age and to allow them to grow with love rather than force. He believed that the heart of a child is like open soil, and whatever is planted early shapes their character for life. He taught that children must be given attention, guidance, and affection. He once explained that a parent who disciplines without warmth harms the spirit, and a parent who loves without boundaries weakens the character. Balance guided his approach, affection joined with wisdom, freedom guided by direction.

Imam Ali believed that children should be raised with three essential gifts: faith, dignity, and knowledge. Faith to ground them, dignity to protect them, and knowledge to empower them. He did not want children to inherit only names or possessions. He wanted them to inherit values, honesty, courage, gratitude, and humility. For him, the greatest inheritance a parent can offer is character.

He taught through example more than instruction. When he helped the poor, his children were beside him. When he forgave an enemy, they witnessed it. When he prayed at night, their hearts absorbed his sincerity. For Imam Ali, parenting was not a series of commands. It was a living demonstration of the values he hoped his children would carry.

He also believed in listening to children. He advised that a wise parent pays attention to the questions and confusions of a child, because within them lie the seeds of their future strengths. He treated his children with respect and never belittled their thoughts or emotions. He believed that children grow confident when they feel heard and valued.

In the realm of extended family, he taught generosity of spirit. He believed that disagreements should be handled with patience and that family ties should be preserved even when pride urges separation. He warned that cutting off family wounds both sides, while healing those ties brings blessing and peace.

Through all of this, he anchored the family in love, not a sentimental or fragile love, but a principled and steady love built on kindness, respect, and shared responsibility. He showed that the home is where the heart is nurtured, where values are shaped, and where human beings learn how to treat the world outside.

Imam Ali taught that anyone who wishes to build a better society must begin by building a better home. If you want children to love truth, let them see truth lived before them. If you want them to be compassionate, let them witness compassion within the walls they call home. If you want them to be courageous, show them what it looks like when a parent stands by what is right.

His teachings on family remain timeless because they speak to human needs that never change: love, dignity, respect, affection, guidance, forgiveness, and presence. They show that greatness does not begin in public life. It begins in the quiet corners of the home, in how people speak, how they listen, how they forgive, and how they love. Imam Ali's home was his first kingdom, and it was there, more than anywhere else, that his nobility shone.

His Vision for Society

Imam Ali did not imagine a world built on conquest, wealth, or domination. His vision was far deeper, more human, and more enduring. He believed that the world improves through fairness, not force; through dignity, not fear; through justice, not spectacle. His idea of society reflected his own character, balanced, compassionate, wise, and grounded in a deep sense of responsibility.

He believed that society must begin with justice. For Imam Ali, justice was not a legal mechanism or an abstract slogan. It was the foundation upon which everything else rests. He taught that no nation survives when injustice spreads through its institutions. Injustice does not remain contained. It grows, moves, and eventually harms the whole community. He believed that leaders must be the first to submit to justice, because when leaders abandon fairness, people lose hope, and when hope disappears, society begins to fracture.

His vision for society rested on the dignity of every human being. He once said that people are of two types: your brother in faith or your equal in humanity. In these few words, he removed the barriers that divide communities and nations. He rejected the idea that faith, tribe, ethnicity, or status should determine a person's worth. To him, every human being was sacred because life itself is a trust from God, and that alone deserved respect.

He believed that society must protect its weakest members. A community's greatness, in his view, was not measured by wealth or monuments, but by how it treated those who struggled. The poor, the orphan, the widow, the laborer, and the traveler were the mirrors in which a society saw its true reflection. He taught that hunger is not only a hardship but also an accusation against those who have the ability to help and choose not to. He believed that no one should sleep hungry in a world that has enough to share.

Imam Ali also believed in economic fairness. He taught that wealth is a trust, not a private treasure. He disapproved of hoarding, corruption, and manipulation. He warned leaders against favoring the wealthy at the expense of the poor and believed that compassion, transparency, and justice must guide societal economy. He recognized the dangers of extreme inequality long before modern economists began to study its effects. In his understanding, when wealth gathers in the hands of a few while the majority suffer, society has already begun to weaken.

He believed that society must be guided by knowledge. Ignorance, more than poverty or weakness, was the true enemy of civilizations. He taught that the mind must be nourished, that education should be available to everyone, and that wisdom is the greatest inheritance one generation can leave to the next. He encouraged learning not only in matters of religion, but in all fields that benefit humanity, including science, language, governance, and ethics. He believed that an educated person sees with two eyes: the eye of intellect and the eye of conscience.

In Imam Ali's vision, society must be built on honesty. He warned that lies weaken trust, and trust is the invisible bond that holds communities together. When trust collapses between leaders and citizens, between neighbors, or between merchants and customers, society becomes fragile. He believed that truth is not always comfortable, but it is always necessary, and he lived by this principle even when it cost him allies.

He believed that society must value humility. A nation ruled by arrogance becomes oppressive. A community led by ego becomes divided. Imam Ali taught leaders to sit with the people, walk among them, and see them not as subjects but as partners in a shared journey. He believed that the powerful must lower themselves so that the weak may rise.

His vision for society also included forgiveness and reconciliation. He understood that communities break apart through conflict, but they heal through mercy. He believed that resentment damages generations, while forgiveness rebuilds them. He taught that unity is worth more than personal victory and that people should not cling to grudges when peace is possible.

He taught that society must treat work with dignity. Every honest laborer, he said, is a partner in building the world, whether they sweep streets or govern cities. He believed that no job is shameful except one done without sincerity. In his vision, society honors workers, pays them fairly, and protects their rights.

He believed that every member of society, no matter how small their role, is essential. Leaders do not build a community alone, but by the collective goodness of ordinary people, the parents raise children with care, the neighbor helping another in need, the merchant who trades honestly, the teacher who shapes young minds, and the youth who chooses integrity over impulse.

Imam Ali's vision for the world was not abstract or unreachable. It was built on clear and practical values: justice, mercy, dignity, humility, knowledge, and honesty. These were not ideas he spoke about from a distance. They were principles he lived every day.

His vision described a world where no one is oppressed, no one is humiliated, no one is ignored, and no one is abandoned. A world where leaders serve instead of dominate. A world where the strong protect the weak, and the weak trust the strong. A world where people remember that humanity is the thread that binds them together.

His Wisdom in Selected Sayings

Imam Ali's wisdom did not grow out of books, debates, or abstract theories. It rose from life itself, from the experiences of a man who was formed inside the household of the Prophet, who witnessed revelation as it unfolded, who stood in moments of danger and hardship, and who carried responsibility while others hesitated. His sayings were not clever lines meant to impress. They were the natural expression of truths he had lived.

From early childhood, Imam Ali was raised in the home of the Prophet Muhammad. During a time of hardship in Mecca, the Prophet took the young Ali into his care, easing the burden on his uncle Abu Talib. From that point forward, Ali grew up beside the Prophet, observing him in every aspect of life. He watched how he spoke, how he treated the weak, how he kept his promises, and how he refused to bow to idols even before the message of Islam was declared openly.

This upbringing shaped the roots of his wisdom. He did not learn faith from distant sermons. He learned it from daily example. When revelation came, Ali did not struggle to believe. He had already seen the truth in the Prophet's character. He accepted the message as a natural continuation of what he had known all his life. His faith was not built on argument but on closeness, trust, and experience.

He followed the Prophet closely, learning from his actions, listening to his words, and carrying his message. He stood beside him in danger, including the night when the Prophet left Mecca for Medina while enemies surrounded his home. Ali slept in the Prophet's bed that night, fully aware of the risk. That courage was not sudden or dramatic. It was the result of a lifetime of loyalty and trust.

All of this formed the foundation of his later sayings. His words were not detached reflections. They were the fruit of a life shaped by the Prophet's presence, tested by hardship, and refined by responsibility.

He once said, "The value of a person is what they do best."

He spoke these words as someone who had grown up in a society obsessed with lineage and status. He had seen noble families act without dignity and poor individuals rise with integrity. In his eyes, a person's worth was not in their ancestry or possessions but in the quality of their actions. This perspective came from the Prophet's home, where dignity was measured by character, not rank.

He often taught that "Silence is the protection of the intelligent."

This lesson came from watching human behavior closely. He saw how arguments erupted from careless speech and how relationships were damaged by impulsive words. He had witnessed the Prophet choose silence over pointless disputes, and he carried that habit into his own life. For him, silence was not weakness. It was clarity, a space where the mind and heart could align.

Another time he said, "Do not know truth by people; know people by truth."

These words reflected the painful years of civil conflict he lived through. He saw tribes follow leaders blindly, attaching themselves to personalities instead of principles. Having grown up under the Prophet, he knew that truth must stand above all individuals. Loyalty to a person without loyalty to truth leads to confusion and injustice.

He said, "He who has no discipline has no honor."

He had watched strong men fail because they could not control themselves. He had seen young warriors lose their potential because they were ruled by impulse. Discipline, in his life, was not a theory. It was the daily practice of someone who prayed at night, worked by day, and restrained himself even when he had the power to act otherwise.

He once said, "Your anger is your enemy; conquer it before it conquers you."

This wisdom came from real moments. He stood in battles where anger could have easily taken control, yet he restrained himself when emotions threatened to cloud justice. His self-control reflected the lessons he absorbed from the Prophet, who showed mercy even in moments of victory.

He taught that "Generosity is giving more than you can, and pride is taking less than you need."

These words describe his own life. He knew poverty firsthand and still gave to others. His generosity was not based on surplus but on compassion. The Prophet's household was one of simplicity, and Ali carried that simplicity into his own life, never allowing wealth to define his worth.

He once told a companion, “If you wish to know the value of the world, look at what it gives to those who love it.”

He had seen people chase power and lose themselves. He had watched greed empty the hearts of those who seemed outwardly successful. From the Prophet, he learned that the world is a place of passage, not permanence. Through this saying, he reminded others not to cling to what cannot last.

Each of Imam Ali’s sayings carries the weight of experience. They were shaped by his childhood beside the Prophet, by the struggles of early Islam, by years of leadership, and by the constant effort to remain sincere in a complicated world. His words speak about pride, anger, justice, discipline, truth, and generosity because he encountered all of them in real life.

His wisdom endures because it is grounded in lived reality. It speaks to struggles that remain unchanged across centuries. Pride still blinds people. Anger still destroys relationships. Wealth still tempts the heart. Truth still stands alone at times. And in each saying, Imam Ali offers not only an observation but a direction. His words are not meant to impress the mind. They are meant to guide the heart.

His Final Lessons Before Martyrdom

As Imam Ali approached the final days of his life, the world around him was tense and divided. Conflicts had shaken the early Muslim community, loyalties had shifted, and wounds, both political and personal, had deepened. In the midst of all this, his own home carried a different atmosphere. There was sorrow in the air, but also calm. He had lived a life of struggle, sacrifice, leadership, and loss, and now he faced his final days with the same steadiness that had marked his entire journey.

On the night he was struck, he had gone to the mosque for the dawn prayer, as was his habit. He had always believed that the house of God was the safest place for the heart, even when the world outside was unsettled. While he was in prayer, he was attacked with a poisoned sword. The blow was severe, and those around him quickly understood the gravity of the moment.

When his sons and companions reached him, they were overwhelmed with grief and fear. But the man they found was not panicking, not cursing, not asking why this had happened. He spoke calmly and with certainty. Among his first recorded words were: "By the Lord of the Kaaba, I have succeeded." These were not the words of someone who felt defeated. They came from a heart that measured life not by survival, but by faithfulness to truth. He believed that a life spent in justice and sincerity was already a victory, no matter how it ended.

He was carried back to his home, wounded and weak, and his family gathered around him. The atmosphere was heavy with emotion. His children saw the condition of their father and could barely hold back their tears. Yet he did not allow despair to fill the room. He spoke to them with tenderness, offering guidance instead of complaints. He reminded them to remain firm in faith, to stay united, and to treat one another with compassion.

In those final hours, he did not speak about power, territory, or unfinished ambitions. He spoke about the poor, the orphans, and the vulnerable. He reminded his family and followers that leadership is a trust, and that the weakest members of society are the true measure of a community's conscience. He urged them to care for those without support, to maintain family ties, and to keep their hearts free from hatred.

His final Will remains one of the most powerful moral documents in early Islamic history. In it, he advised his sons to be mindful of God in all matters, to stand firmly with truth, and to avoid oppression under any circumstance. He told them that the world often deceives those who become attached to it, and that life moves quickly, leaving only deeds behind. These were not abstract teachings. They were the summary of a life he had already lived.

Even in his wounded state, he refused to let anger dictate his instructions. He spoke about the man who had attacked him and told his family that if he survived, he would decide the matter himself. If he did not survive, they were to treat the attacker with justice and nothing more. He made it clear that no cruelty, no excess, and no revenge should be carried out in his name. His body was in pain, but his principles remained untouched.

He reminded his children to guard their hearts against arrogance, explaining that pride blinds the soul and distances a person from truth. He urged them to practice patience, not as passive endurance but as strength that keeps the heart stable during hardship. He told them to hold tightly to truthfulness, because truth keeps a person close to God, even when the world turns away.

In his final advice, he gave words that reflect the essence of his entire life. He told them to fear God and not to chase the world if it turned away from them, nor to cling to it if it came toward them. He wanted their hearts to remain free, not tied to possessions or status. He asked them to fill their hearts with compassion for people, because compassion is what makes a human being noble.

Then he gave a statement that has echoed through centuries: be a helper of the oppressed and an opponent of the oppressor. This was not a slogan or a dramatic line meant for effect. It was the core of his character. He had lived by these words in battle, in leadership, in judgment, and in private life.

When Imam Ali left the world, he did not leave behind palaces, monuments, or treasures. He left a moral legacy. He left a model of courage without cruelty, authority without arrogance, and faith without harshness. His children carried that legacy, as did his students, his admirers, and generations who found strength in his example.

His final lessons were not commands shouted from a throne. They were the gentle guidance of a father, a leader, and a servant of God, offered in the quiet hours before his departure. They were expressions of love, shaped into advice, left behind as a path for anyone who seeks to live with dignity, compassion, and truth.

His Words to the World Today

If Imam Ali could speak directly to the world today, a world that is confused, tired, divided, searching, his message would not be complicated. It would be simple, human, and clear, just as his teachings always were. His words would not be for one group or one belief. They would be for every heart that still feels, still hopes, still longs for a better life.

He would tell the world to return to justice, not the justice written in laws alone, but the justice lived in daily actions. He would remind leaders that their responsibility is sacred, that the people they serve are not numbers but souls, and that every wound caused by injustice returns eventually to the one who inflicted it. He would tell the world's powerful that pride is the beginning of downfall and humility is the beginning of wisdom.

He would tell societies to treat every human being with dignity. He would say again what he said centuries ago:

> "People are either your brother in faith,
> or your equal in humanity."

He would remind nations that the world becomes smaller every day, and only compassion can hold it together.

He would tell families to build their homes on respect, love, and patience. He would remind parents that children learn more from character than correction. He would remind spouses that gentleness is strength, not weakness. He would ask people to speak to each other kindly, for every heart is fighting a battle unseen.

He would tell human beings not to let anger guide their lives. He would teach them to pause before reacting, to breathe before speaking, and to think before judging. He would remind them that a moment of anger can destroy what years of love built.

He would tell the oppressed not to lose hope. He would remind them that no injustice lasts forever and that God's eyes never close. He would tell them that every tear shed in silence, every prayer whispered in pain, every truth spoken without support becomes a seed that one day transforms the world.

He would tell the oppressor to stop, not for fear of punishment, but for fear of losing their own soul. He would remind them that power is temporary, that pride is blinding, and that the cries of victims rise louder than any throne can silence.

He would tell the world to forgive whenever possible, not to forget, not to excuse, but to free the heart from bitterness. He would remind humanity that forgiveness heals the giver before the recipient.

He would tell seekers of meaning to look within. He would remind them that the heart is the lantern of the soul, and the soul is guided not by noise but by sincerity. He would ask them to feed their spirit with knowledge, reflection, and goodness.

And finally, he would tell every person, no matter who they are, no matter where they stand, that the path to a noble life is always open. That greatness is not written in birth, wealth, or status, but in the quiet choices made every day. He would remind humanity that the smallest act of kindness ripples through generations and that the pure intention whispered to God is never lost.

If Imam Ali could speak to the world today, he would not demand worship or praise. He would ask the world to become decent again, to become honest again, to become compassionate again, to become brave again, to become human again.

And he would leave the world with the same message he left his children in his final will:

“Fear God, honor humanity, stand with the oppressed, speak the truth, and let your hearts be filled with compassion.”

This is his message, timeless, gentle, and powerful, a lantern for every soul that seeks the light.

His Impact on Future Generations

When Imam Ali left this world, his body returned to the earth, but his presence did not disappear. It began to move through history in a different form. His life became a reference point, a memory that did not fade with time. Instead, it grew stronger with each generation that returned to his words and reflected on his example. He was no longer walking among people, but people kept walking toward him.

The first to carry his legacy were those who had lived beside him. His children, his companions, and his students did not remember him as a distant ruler or a figure wrapped in ceremony. They remembered the man who spoke gently, who listened with attention, who shared their hardships, and who never placed himself above others. They spoke of his courage, but also of his tenderness. They remembered how he comforted the distressed, how he fed the poor, and how he prayed with sincerity when no one was watching. Their memories were not legends. They were lived experiences, and through them, the first seeds of his legacy were planted.

Those seeds soon found their way into the minds of scholars and thinkers. His sermons, letters, and judgments became material for reflection and study. Jurists examined his rulings and found a balance between law and mercy. Philosophers read his sayings and discovered a deep understanding of the human soul. His letter to Malik al-Ashtar was studied as a guide for ethical governance, a document that spoke of justice, humility, accountability, and compassion long before such ideas were organized into modern political theories. His words were not treated as relics of the past. They were used as tools for shaping the future.

As the Muslim world expanded, the memory of Imam Ali traveled with it. In Persia, poets found in him the image of a warrior whose sword served justice and whose heart belonged to God. His character entered verses and stories, becoming a symbol of honor and sincerity. In the Indian subcontinent, scholars studied his legal judgments as examples of fairness. In Arab lands, his bravery became a model of dignity. In parts of Africa and Central Asia, stories of his humility and simplicity inspired leaders and ordinary people alike. His life crossed languages and cultures because the values he lived by were not tied to one place.

Spiritual teachers also looked to him as a guide. Many Sufi traditions traced their teachings back to him, seeing in him a man who combined strength of action with depth of spirit. They believed he had inherited the inner wisdom of the Prophet and passed it down through both word and example. Through their circles, his teachings reached remote regions and touched people who knew little about early Islamic history but felt drawn to the clarity and compassion in his words.

Outside the Muslim world, historians and moral thinkers encountered his life and found themselves impressed by his character. Some European writers described him as the model of chivalry, a man who carried both courage and mercy in equal measure. Others saw in him an example of leadership grounded in conscience rather than ambition. Even those who did not share his faith could recognize the rare balance in his personality, strength without cruelty, authority without pride, and devotion without harshness.

Still, the deepest impact of Imam Ali did not belong to scholars, poets, or rulers. It lived in the daily lives of ordinary people. Parents repeated his sayings to their children. Teachers shared his advice with their students. Workers, merchants, and travelers carried stories of his fairness and generosity. A widow who once received food in the night without knowing the giver told her children about the mysterious helper who later turned out to be their leader. A man who saw him forgive an enemy passed that story to his grandchildren. In this way, his presence moved quietly from one heart to another.

With time, he became a measure by which people judged leadership. When rulers lived in luxury while their people suffered, the memory of Imam Ali's simple life stood in contrast. When judges twisted the law to favor the powerful, people remembered the story of how he accepted a court decision against himself rather than misuse his authority. His life became a mirror, one that every generation could look into and see both its shortcomings and its possibilities.

His influence also reached beyond religious identity. He shaped ideals that entered the human conscience itself. Justice, humility, courage, compassion, and integrity, these were not merely religious virtues. They were human ones. And because he embodied them with balance and sincerity, his life became a universal reference point for moral character.

In every era, people returned to him not because they were required to, but because they found something in him that they longed for. They saw in him the kind of leader they wished existed. They saw in him the kind of person they hoped to become. His life was free of the hypocrisy that often stains public figures. It was marked by consistency, from his youth beside the Prophet to his final breath.

His impact endures because the truths he spoke are not bound to a century. His values do not grow old, and his wisdom does not lose its light. He addressed the human condition itself, and that condition remains the same across time.

His legacy lives in the human longing for justice, kindness, clarity, and dignity. It lives in the quiet hope that the world can be better than it is. It lives in the hearts of those who see in Imam Ali not only a figure from history, but a companion for the present. He left the world centuries ago, but the world has never managed to leave him behind.

When Integrity Refused Compromise

There are moments in history when a leader is forced to choose between what is easy and what is right. These are the moments that reveal the true measure of a human being. For Imam Ali, the conflict with the governor of Syria was not simply a political disagreement. It was a test of conscience, a moment where integrity stood face to face with expediency.

When Imam Ali assumed leadership (the calapha), the Muslim world was already wounded by unrest and tension. The assassination of the previous caliph had left the community divided and suspicious. Some leaders demanded immediate retaliation against those responsible. Others called for patience, investigation, and fairness. Among those who refused allegiance was the governor of Syria, who insisted that justice for the slain caliph must come before any recognition of the new leader.

Imam Ali to protect he nation from further divide did not reject the demand for justice. He believed deeply in it. But he also understood that justice cannot grow out of chaos, nor can it be built on anger. The situation in the capital was unstable. The identities of the killers were mixed with political factions and tribal rivalries. Acting in haste would not bring justice. It would only deepen the bloodshed.

He refused to punish people without clear evidence. He refused to act out of pressure. He refused to trade principle for political gain. Some advised him to make temporary compromises, to keep certain governors in power even if they were known for injustice and corruption, just to maintain stability. Others suggested that he delay reforms until his authority was secure.

He refused all of it.

He believed that leadership begins with honesty. If the foundation is crooked, the building will never stand straight. He could not preach justice while preserving corrupt systems. He could not ask people to trust him while keeping unjust officials in power. So he chose the harder path, the path of immediate reform, even if it cost him political support.

The governor of Syria used the demand for revenge as a political banner. He gathered supporters, refused allegiance, and eventually led his region into open opposition. The tension escalated into a military confrontation. It was a tragic moment, not because of the clash itself, but because it represented a fracture within the same community.

Throughout the conflict, Imam Ali's conduct never descended into cruelty or manipulation. He did not spread lies about his opponent. He did not use deceit to gain advantage. He did not exploit religion to inflame hatred. He kept reminding his followers that their opponents were still fellow believers, not enemies to be destroyed.

He instructed his soldiers not to start the fighting. He forbade them from harming civilians. He ordered them not to mutilate bodies, not to pursue those who fled, and not to deny water to the opposing army, even when his own men had gained control of the river and wells. To him, war was never a license for brutality.

At one point during the conflict, negotiations nearly brought peace. But political maneuvering and emotional appeals prolonged the struggle. Many around him urged him to use similar tactics, to match strategy with strategy, deception with deception. He refused.

He said that victory gained through falsehood is not a true victory. He would rather lose power than lose his conscience. He would rather stand with truth and be abandoned than gather supporters through manipulation.

This refusal cost him dearly. Some followers grew frustrated with his moral restraint. Others were swayed by political propaganda. The conflict drained his resources, weakened his authority, and deepened divisions in the community. From a purely political perspective, compromise might have secured his position.

But Imam Ali was not interested in power for its own sake. He once said that authority meant nothing to him unless it allowed him to establish justice or remove oppression. Leadership, in his eyes, was a responsibility.

At every crossroads, he chose integrity over advantage. He chose fairness over speed. He chose truth over strategy. He chose conscience over control.

He could have delayed reforms. He could have negotiated

power-sharing arrangements that preserved unjust officials. He could have used propaganda or tribal loyalties to secure his rule. Many rulers before and after him did exactly that. It would have been considered normal politics. But he refused to build an alliance on compromised values.

His stance offers a powerful lesson to every age. Leadership is often tested not by enemies, but by opportunities to compromise. The temptation to bend principles for stability, popularity, or short-term success appears in every generation. Many leaders accept it. They justify it. They call it pragmatism.

Imam Ali called it betrayal of the soul.

He showed that integrity is not proven when things are easy. It is proven when compromise offers comfort and conscience demands sacrifice. His refusal to trade justice for political advantage is what gives his leadership its enduring moral authority.

History remembers many rulers who expanded territories, built monuments, and accumulated wealth. But their legacies faded with time. Imam Ali's legacy endured not because he won every conflict, but because he never lost himself. When integrity refused compromise, he chose integrity.

And in that choice, he secured a victory far greater than any political triumph. He secured the respect of history, the admiration of scholars, and the love of millions who continue to see in him a leader who proved that power without principle is empty, but principle without power can still change the world.

A Message to the Modern Heart

In a time when the world feels overwhelmed by noise, division, speed, injustice, and a quiet loneliness hidden beneath technology, the teachings of Imam Ali enter like a deep breath. His life, once lived in deserts and early cities, now speaks with surprising clarity to modern humans sitting in office buildings, crowded streets, quiet bedrooms, or restless hearts. He matters today because what he stood for is exactly what the world is searching for: integrity, compassion, courage, fairness, and meaning.

We live in an age where truth often feels negotiable, where appearances carry more weight than character, where leadership is mistaken for loudness, and where justice sometimes feels distant. Imam Ali becomes relevant not because of nostalgia, but because he offers something the present world struggles to produce: sincerity. His life shows what it means to live without duplicity, to speak without manipulation, and to lead without ego. In a time when many are disillusioned with leaders, his example stands as proof that ethical leadership is not a fantasy. It has existed, and it can exist again.

He matters today because people are searching for emotional and spiritual grounding. Modern life moves quickly, carries heavy expectations, and leaves many feeling uncertain. Anxiety and exhaustion have become quiet companions for countless people. Imam Ali spoke to the restlessness of the human heart long before modern psychology gave it labels.

He taught patience that strengthens rather than suppresses, courage that steadies rather than rushes, humility that frees rather than diminishes, and hope that rises through pain rather than denying it. His wisdom reaches those who feel overwhelmed, reminding them that endurance is not weakness and that wounds can become lights that guide the way forward.

He matters today because societies across the world continue to wrestle with injustice, economic inequality, discrimination, corruption, and abuse of power. Imam Ali's voice speaks clearly across the centuries: "Be a helper of the oppressed and an enemy of the oppressor." He did not say this for applause or poetry. He lived it. He refused to take what was not his, refused to favor those with wealth, and refused to ignore the cries of the poor. When modern societies demand fairness, transparency, and equality, they are calling for the same values he lived with unwavering clarity.

He matters today because ordinary people still search for guidance on how to live good lives, how to love with sincerity, raise children with wisdom, forgive old wounds, balance ambition with humility, and walk through the world with dignity. Imam Ali's teachings offer a map. They show how to be strong without harshness, gentle without weakness, generous without being exploited, and truthful without cruelty. He teaches not only how to act in public, but how to behave in private, when no one is watching.

He matters today because the modern world often confuses convenience with morality. Many seek shortcuts to success and comfort. Imam Ali taught that character is built through discipline, self-control, fairness, and kindness. He reminded people that success built dishonestly collapses quickly, and that a meaningful life is not a life of shortcuts but a life of sincerity.

He matters because he understood human relationships with deep clarity. He knew that friendships shape destiny, that words can build or destroy hearts, and that arrogance ruins more blessings than failure ever could. He understood that love requires gentleness, that family requires patience, and that forgiveness frees the soul more than punishment ever will.

He matters because countless people today feel unseen, unheard, and undervalued. Imam Ali spoke directly to them when he said that every person is either your brother in faith or your equal in humanity. In a divided world, his vision restores dignity. In a world full of labels, he reminds people of their shared humanity. In a world shaped by conflict, he calls for compassion.

He matters because the essence of his life rises above religion, politics, or time. His message is not limited to one community. It speaks to the human being. It reminds every reader that greatness is not measured by wealth, fame, or power, but by the condition of the heart and the integrity of the soul.

He matters today because the world is searching for real examples of goodness in action. People have grown tired of speeches without substance. They look for sincerity, not performance; character, not image; proven hearts, not promises.

Imam Ali's heart was tested in every way a human heart can be tested, through loss, betrayal, conflict, responsibility, love, and sacrifice, and it remained steady. He became a living example of ethical strength.

That is why he matters today. Because he offers the world what it cannot easily produce on its own. He shows that truth still exists, that justice is possible, that humility is strength, that compassion is power, and that nobility remains within human reach. He reminds us that one sincere heart, guided by conscience, can still transform the world around it.

Imam Ali's Timeless Model of Courage

Strength Without Cruelty, Bravery Without Arrogance

Courage is often misunderstood. Many imagine it as something loud, forceful, and dramatic, a charge forward, a raised voice, a bold declaration. But Imam Ali revealed a different kind of courage, one that remains rare in every era. His courage grew from a clean heart, a steady mind, and a soul anchored in truth. It was not the courage of impulse, but the courage of clarity. Not the courage of anger, but the courage of dignity. Not the courage of showmanship, but of sincerity.

His courage began long before the battlefield. It began when he was a young boy, among the first to stand with the Prophet when others hesitated. While many adults paused in uncertainty, he stepped forward with loyalty and conviction. That courage deepened on the night of the migration, when he slept in the Prophet's bed knowing that assassins surrounded the house. He understood the danger. He did not deny it or pretend it was not there. He simply chose loyalty over fear. His courage came from the belief that protecting what is right is worth more than protecting one's comfort.

On the battlefield, his bravery became widely known. Warriors hesitated to face him, not because he was cruel, but because he was disciplined. He fought with restraint, precision, and purpose. When he disarmed an opponent, he did not strike out of rage. There is a well-known account in which he overpowered an enemy in combat, and when the man insulted him, he stepped back rather than kill him. He refused to let anger dictate his actions. His courage never crossed the line into cruelty. He did not mutilate bodies, did not pursue the wounded, and did not allow hatred to shape his conduct. This was strength governed by conscience.

Even more striking was his moral courage. Many people can show bravery when holding a weapon, but far fewer can stand firm in truth when surrounded by pressure. Imam Ali did not flatter those in power, nor did he soften his principles to gain support. He spoke the truth even when it cost him allies, comfort, and stability. His courage did not come from pride. It came from an inner awareness that refused to compromise what was right. He often reminded people that the strongest person is not the one who conquers others, but the one who conquers their own impulses.

His courage also appeared in forgiveness. It takes nerve to strike an enemy, but it takes deeper strength to forgive one. He forgave those who insulted him, betrayed him, or abandoned him. He did not forgive because he lacked power. He forgave because he possessed control over his ego. He understood that revenge burdens the heart, while forgiveness frees it.

Patience was another form of courage in his life. There were moments when confusion surrounded him, when people misunderstood him, and when truth was distorted by politics and ambition. During such times, he did not panic or lose his balance. He endured with steadiness. This, too, is courage, the ability to remain principled when disappointment or injustice presses heavily on the heart.

The modern world often celebrates loudness, aggression, and domination as signs of bravery. Imam Ali offers a different image. He shows that real courage is the ability to stand with truth when it is unpopular, to walk away from cruelty when cruelty is easy, to rise after betrayal without becoming bitter, and to carry responsibility without arrogance.

His courage remains timeless because it is rooted in character, not circumstance. It does not depend on armies, weapons, or titles. It depends on the strength of the heart, a strength available to any person who chooses sincerity over ego and justice over convenience.

This is why his courage continues to inspire. It reminds humanity that bravery is not about overpowering others. It is about mastering oneself.

The Eternal Reflection of Imam Ali

When people read about Imam Ali, they often begin with admiration, his courage, his wisdom, his loyalty, his justice. But something deeper happens as the pages turn. The admiration quietly shifts into recognition. The reader begins to see that he is not only a figure to appreciate, but a mirror that reveals the inner landscape of the human soul.

Every value he embodied, honesty, compassion, bravery, patience, humility, awakens something inside us, a truth we sometimes ignore or forget. He shows us not who we are now, but who we could be if we chose sincerity over pride, clarity over confusion, and goodness over convenience. In this way, Imam Ali becomes less of a historical character and more of a reflection that illuminates our strengths, exposes our weaknesses, and calls us toward our better selves.

When we read about his justice, we are forced to ask whether our own decisions are fair. When we read about his courage, we question how much of our fear guides us. When we read about his compassion, we wonder if we have overlooked those who needed us. When we read about his humility, we confront the parts of ourselves that crave attention and praise. When we read about his patience, we see how easily we lose ours. When we read about his forgiveness, we are invited to release the anger we have carried for years.

He does not judge us. He simply shows us the difference between what we admire and what we practice. And in that space, a new desire is born, the desire to grow.

For some, Imam Ali reveals the strength they have hidden beneath self-doubt. For others, he reveals the clarity lost under the noise of life. For many, he reveals the part of the heart that still believes in goodness, decency, fairness, and humanity.

In a world where people often feel pulled in many directions, Imam Ali becomes a compass. He points inward first, reminding each person that the greatest victories happen inside the heart, taming anger, rising above jealousy, resisting cruelty, speaking truth gently, showing kindness quietly. These are the battles no one sees, yet they build the character everyone admires.

He also reveals our longing for integrity. People today do not lack information; they lack examples. They lack people whose words match their actions, whose strength never sacrifices kindness, and whose leadership never abandons ethics. In him, the reader finds exactly that kind of human being. And suddenly, the distance between admiration and aspiration disappears.

Imam Ali does not make the reader feel small. He makes the reader feel possible. He shows that nobility is not inherited, it is lived. He shows that greatness is not a gift, it is a discipline. He shows that light is not found elsewhere; it is cultivated within.

Many who read about him discover that they want to imitate not his victories, but his virtues. They want his clarity in confusion, his discipline in temptation, his calmness under pressure, his fairness when tested, his compassion when wronged. And in that desire, the reader discovers a truth: humanity has not changed as much as we imagine. Our hearts still yearn for the same qualities that he embodied centuries ago.

In this way, Imam Ali becomes the reflection of the soul, revealing not only who he was, but who we are capable of becoming. The reader feels it: a soft pull toward something higher, a longing to refine their own character, a quiet awakening that whispers, "You, too, can live nobly."

This is perhaps his greatest gift. He does not stand above humanity; he elevates humanity. He does not ask us to worship him; he inspires us to improve ourselves. He does not overwhelm the mind; he awakens the conscience.

In seeing him, we begin to see ourselves, not in who we are today, but in who we could be tomorrow. That is why his reflection is eternal. Because every generation needs someone who reminds it of its best self. And Imam Ali does so not with force, but with example. Not with fear, but with wisdom. Not by demanding devotion, but by showing what a noble human life looks like when lived with sincerity, courage, and compassion.

Was Imam Ali the Perfect Human Being?

History remembers Imam Ali for his courage, his wisdom, his justice, and his leadership. But to understand who he truly was, one must move closer, beyond the battlefield, beyond the pulpit, beyond the seat of authority he never chased. At his core, Imam Ali was deeply human. He felt the weight of life, the pain of others, the responsibility of leadership, and the tenderness of love. His greatness did not grow from distance or mystery. It grew from a life lived in full contact with the realities of ordinary people.

As a leader of the nation, he repaired his own clothes. He patched his own sandals. He carried water to his home and shared his food with the poor, even when his own portion was small. He walked through the marketplace without guards or grand displays. He greeted people with humility, spoke gently to children, and listened to the worries of those who approached him. People did not feel intimidated in his presence. They felt seen. They felt heard. His character comforted hearts before his wisdom even reached the mind.

He wept in prayer, not as a display, but from a heart that felt the weight of the world. He feared injustice more than he feared death. He cried for orphans and widows, not as a ruler fulfilling a duty, but as a human being whose heart could not remain still in the face of suffering. His emotions were never hidden behind a mask of authority. He transformed them into compassion and service. That humanity made people trust him, love him, and feel safe in his presence.

He knew loneliness. He felt betrayal. He endured hardships that would have broken many others. But he never allowed bitterness to take root in his heart. When friends turned into opponents, he remained fair. When others spoke against him, he chose restraint. When leadership was delayed from him, he accepted it with dignity. When conflict became unavoidable, he entered it without thirst for victory. He fought because he had to, not because he wanted to. That restraint came from a depth of character, not from weakness.

He could stand fearlessly in battle and still give away his last piece of bread to someone in need. He could debate scholars with clarity and then sit on the ground beside a child as if nothing else in the world mattered. He could lead armies and still sweep the floor of the mosque with his own hands. There was no contradiction in him. The same man appeared in every place, the same heart, the same conscience, the same simplicity.

He worried about people. He paid attention to the vulnerable. He spoke often about the state of the heart rather than the size of one's power. He believed the human being was a noble creation of God and therefore deserved dignity, fairness, and compassion. His humanity was not separate from his greatness. It was the source of it.

He was human in his tenderness, human in his struggles, human in his humility, human in his patience, and human in his love. Because of that, people recognized themselves in him. They saw their fears, their hopes, their weaknesses, and their longing for meaning reflected in his life.

He reminds us that being human is not a limitation. It is the beginning of all nobility.

That dignity grows from sincerity, not perfection. That strength is measured not by the volume of one's commands, but by the steadiness of one's justice. That greatness is open to anyone whose heart remains clean, whose intentions remain honest, and whose actions reflect truth.

In the end, it is his humanity that gives his legacy its power. It shows that the qualities people admire in him are not distant ideals. They are choices, choices available to every person, in every place, in every age.

He was a caliph, a leader, a warrior, a scholar, and a saint. But before all of that, he was a human being. A man whose heart felt deeply, whose conscience spoke clearly, and whose soul moved gently through a harsh world. And it is this humanity that continues to guide, inspire, and awaken hearts across the centuries.

Imam Ali's Love for Humanity

Imam Ali's love for humanity was not an abstract idea or a distant principle. It was something people could feel in his presence, hear in his voice, and witness in his actions. His love did not come from soft words or noble speeches alone. It grew from a deep understanding of the human soul, its fragility, its confusion, its longing, and its capacity for goodness.

He did not see people as ranks, tribes, or categories. He saw them as human beings created with dignity. When he said, "People are of two types: your brothers in faith or your equals in humanity," he was not offering a philosophical statement. He was expressing a way of seeing the world. In those words, he removed the barriers that divide people and replaced them with a single truth: every human being carries worth.

His compassion was born from his ability to feel the pain of others. When he saw poverty, he felt responsible. When he witnessed injustice, it disturbed his heart. When he heard the cry of a widow, he could not sleep in comfort. When he met an orphan, he treated the child as his own. He once expressed that if a person went hungry under his authority, he considered it a wound on his own soul. This was not political language. It was a reflection of how deeply he cared.

His love appeared in his judgments. He did not allow anger to cloud justice, and he never allowed favoritism to enter his decisions. The powerful and the weak stood before him as equals. He reminded leaders that fairness is the foundation of any healthy society. His kindness was not selective. It reached strangers, opponents, and even the man who struck him. Where the world expected harshness, he answered with restraint and dignity.

He believed the human being was a trust. Every person, in his view, deserved honesty, compassion, and respect. He believed education should be available to all, that hunger was an injustice, and that cruelty violated not only morality but humanity itself. He warned against filling the heart with hatred. He taught people to treat others as they themselves wished to be treated, not as a rule, but as a natural expression of conscience.

His love for humanity was generous, patient, and sincere. It came from faith, but also from life itself. He had walked beside the Prophet, witnessed the struggles of the poor, fought for justice, and endured hardship without bitterness. Each experience shaped a heart that saw goodness where others saw weakness, potential where others saw failure, and unity where others saw division.

His love endures not because it belongs to the past, but because it answers the needs of the present. In an age marked by conflict, loneliness, and fear, his compassion becomes a guiding light. It reminds us that humanity is not lost. It only waits for hearts brave enough to care for it again.

The Lasting Example of Balance

In a time when many families struggle to remain connected, when homes are filled with distraction instead of presence, and when relationships often feel rushed, the household of Imam Ali offers a lasting example of balance, affection, and shared purpose. His home was modest in size, but rich in warmth. Its walls were simple, but its values were deep.

The first lesson is partnership. Imam Ali and Fatima shared their struggles, responsibilities, and hopes. Their marriage was not built on control or status, but on companionship. They saw each other as partners walking the same path, not as rivals or distant figures under the same roof. Their relationship showed that unity grows through cooperation, kindness, and mutual respect.

The second lesson is presence. In a world where attention is scattered and time feels scarce, Imam Ali gave his children what every child longs for: his presence. He did not offer wealth or luxury. He offered himself. He listened to their questions, guided their thinking, comforted their fears, and shaped their hearts. He showed that true parenting is not about providing things, but about shaping character.

The third lesson is values. Hasan, Husayn, Zaynab, and Umm Kulthum were raised with clarity of character. They were taught humility, courage, patience, generosity, and truthfulness. These values became their strength in later trials.

Many parents today struggle to raise children in a noisy and unstable world. Imam Ali's example shows that grounding a child in character prepares them better for life than any material success.

The fourth lesson is gentleness. Despite the burdens of leadership and the storms of political conflict around him, he did not bring harshness into his home. He treated his children with tenderness and Fatima with deep respect. His home was a place of peace, not an extension of the world's pressures. In many modern households, stress, and exhaustion spill into daily life. His example reminds us that a home must remain a refuge.

The fifth lesson is shared faith and purpose. His family prayed together, learned together, and supported one another through hardship. They understood that faith was not limited to rituals. It was a way of living. They met sorrow with patience and success with humility. Families searching for meaning today can learn from this unity, that a shared purpose strengthens the bond between hearts.

Imam Ali's family did not live in wealth. They experienced hardship and loss. But their bond remained strong because it was built on sincerity, love, and mutual care. In their example, the modern world finds a blueprint for homes that nurture rather than exhaust, homes that lift the spirit rather than drain it, homes where love is practiced, not merely spoken.

The world has changed in its technology and culture, but the human need for warmth, trust, dignity, and belonging remains the same. The family of Imam Ali offers a model that reaches across time, reminding us that the strongest homes are not built on wealth, but on love.

A Model for Every Civilization

When we gather the moments of Imam Ali's life, the courage of his youth, the loyalty of his adulthood, the justice of his leadership, the tenderness of his heart, the brilliance of his mind, and the humility that held it all together, a full portrait begins to appear. It is not shaped by exaggeration or legend, but by a steady character that remained consistent through every stage of his life. He lived as though truth was the only path worth taking and compassion, the only language worth speaking.

In his life, strength and gentleness existed together without conflict. Imam Ali was a warrior who never loved violence, a leader who chose simplicity over comfort, a thinker who acted with clarity, and a spiritual man who remained close to the struggles of ordinary people. Others spent their lives building reputations. He spent his life building character. Others gathered followers. He gathered principles. Others chased authority. He chased sincerity. There was no split between his words and his actions, and that is why his name traveled through centuries with respect.

He did not become a model because he demanded admiration. He became one because he lived in a way that made imitation natural. His life did not ask for praise. It offered direction. His actions did not claim perfection. They reflected integrity. Everything he taught, he practiced. Everything he advised and preached; he lived. Everything he believed in, he carried with him until his final breath.

For the young, Imam Ali's courage becomes a guide, showing that bravery is not loud, but loyal. For the elders, his wisdom becomes a companion, reminding them that experience should soften the heart, not harden it. For leaders, his justice becomes a reminder, revealing the difference between power and responsibility. For the oppressed, his endurance becomes a source of dignity, showing that honor can survive even the harshest trials.

For families, his gentleness becomes a lesson, proving that strength is best expressed through kindness. For seekers of meaning, his spirituality becomes a light that points inward, toward the place where truth speaks quietly to the heart. And for those who feel lost, he becomes a steady reference, balanced, compassionate, and clear.

Imam Ali's final image is not made from a single quality. It is formed from many layers, courage shaped by hardship, patience shaped by sacrifice, love softened by humility, and wisdom deepened by experience. The portrait feels alive because it reflects the fullness of the human journey.

He understood suffering because he lived through betrayal, battles, poverty, loss, and long periods of isolation. He understood love because he shared a home with the Prophet's daughter and raised children whose hearts carried his light.

He understood struggle because he tried to guide a community that did not always understand him. He understood the inner life because his nights were spent in reflection and his days in service.

Through all of this, he remained steady. He did not bend his principles to gain approval. He did not trade justice for popularity. He did not abandon compassion when the world became harsh. His character held together through every storm.

What makes Imam Ali a model for every age is not what he achieved, but how he lived. He did not build empires. He built people. He did not collect wealth. He collected wisdom. He did not conquer lands. He conquered the ego. He did not demand loyalty. He inspired it. He did not chase greatness. Greatness found him in the way he lived.

Every generation that discovers him finds something of itself in his life. The world changes, but the human heart does not. The heart still longs for fairness, sincerity, love, meaning, and dignity. Imam Ali stands at the meeting point of all these longings.

His image remains timeless because it speaks directly to the human condition. It reminds the reader that a life built on sincerity does not fade with time. It grows stronger with every generation that encounters it.

The Image of Imam Ali is not meant to be admired from a distance. It is meant to inspire movement. It invites each reader to carry even a small portion of his compassion, his clarity, his humility, and his courage into their own life.

If his image leaves one message for every age, it is simple.

Be a human being whose character becomes your legacy. Be a soul whose integrity outlives your years. Be a heart that adds light to the world instead of darkness.

This is what Imam Ali represents. This is why he endures. The final image of Imam Ali reveals a great human being who lived with sincerity, humility, and moral clarity until the end.

Voices from Across Traditions and Civilizations

Imam Ali was not remembered only by those who loved him, followed him, or belonged to his tradition. His character reached beyond sect, beyond geography, beyond time. People from different religions, cultures, and intellectual traditions looked at his life and saw something rare. They saw a human being whose actions aligned with his words, whose courage did not erase his compassion, and whose authority did not weaken his humility.

What is remarkable is not that his followers praised him. That is natural. What is remarkable is how many people outside his circle, sometimes even outside his faith, spoke about him with admiration and respect.

George Jordac (Lebanese Christian writer)

George Jordac devoted years of his life to studying Imam Ali's words, especially those preserved in *Nahj al-Balagha*. He eventually wrote a multi-volume work titled *Imam Ali: The Voice of Human Justice*. Jordac did not approach Imam Ali as a believer or a sectarian writer. He approached him as a literary and philosophical figure. After studying his speeches and letters, Jordac concluded that Imam Ali represented one of the greatest models of justice in human history. He wrote that if Imam Ali's principles of governance were applied in the modern world, humanity would witness a new era of dignity and fairness. For Jordac, Imam Ali was not a figure of one religion. He was a universal voice of justice.

Khalil Gibran (Lebanese Christian poet and philosopher)

Khalil Gibran, the renowned author of *The Prophet*, wrote about Imam Ali with deep admiration. He described him as a man who died before his message was fully understood by his people. Gibran saw in him a figure whose soul was too advanced for his time, someone whose inner life carried a depth that his society could not fully absorb. In Gibran's eyes, Imam Ali was a human being whose spirit belonged to a higher moral plane.

Sarvepalli Radhakrishnan (Indian philosopher and former President of India)

Radhakrishnan, one of the most respected philosophers of the twentieth century, referred to Imam Ali as one of the noblest figures produced by humanity. He recognized in him a rare harmony between intellect and moral courage. Radhakrishnan saw Imam Ali not simply as a religious figure, but as a universal ethical personality whose life offered lessons to all civilizations.

Mahatma Gandhi (Indian leader)

Gandhi studied the lives of several religious and ethical figures across traditions. He is reported to have admired Imam Ali's sense of justice and his commitment to truth, especially in difficult political circumstances. Gandhi saw in Imam Ali a model of principled leadership, one who refused to compromise his moral standards for political gain. For

Gandhi, Imam Ali's life reflected the idea that true leadership must be rooted in ethical conviction rather than force.

Wilferd Madelung (German historian of Islam)

In his academic work *The Succession to Muhammad*, Madelung portrayed Imam Ali as a man whose claim to leadership was deeply connected to moral merit and closeness to the Prophet. His analysis, though scholarly and historical rather than devotional, showed respect for Imam Ali's integrity, knowledge, and character. Madelung emphasized that Imam Ali represented a model of principled leadership in early Islamic history.

Marshall G. S. Hodgson (American historian)

In *The Venture of Islam*, Hodgson described Imam Ali as a deeply respected figure, even among those who opposed him politically. He noted the admiration people held for his courage, honesty, and devotion. Hodgson presented him as a central moral personality in Islamic civilization, someone whose character shaped the ethical imagination of later generations.

Ibn Abi al-Hadid (Mu'tazili scholar, Baghdad)

Ibn Abi al-Hadid, though not a Shi'i scholar, wrote one of the most extensive commentaries on *Nahj al-Balagha*. He described Imam Ali as a personality whose virtues filled every aspect of life. He admired his knowledge, courage, generosity, and moral clarity. Ibn Abi al-Hadid wrote that all virtues seemed to gather in Imam Ali, as if he were their natural home.

Al-Shafi'i (Sunni jurist and founder of the Shafi'i school)

Imam al-Shafi'i spoke with respect about Imam Ali's knowledge and virtue. He is reported to have said that whenever he faced a legal difficulty, he turned to the sayings of Imam Ali. For al-Shafi'i, Imam Ali represented a deep reservoir of knowledge and moral understanding.

Ahmad ibn Hanbal (Sunni scholar and founder of the Hanbali school)

Ahmad ibn Hanbal included numerous reports about the virtues of Imam Ali in his works. He stated that no companion of the Prophet had as many authentic reports about his virtues as Imam Ali. This was not a sectarian statement. It came from a leading Sunni authority who recognized the exceptional place Imam Ali held among the companions.

Al-Tabari (early Muslim historian)

In his monumental historical chronicle, al-Tabari preserved many reports describing Imam Ali's courage, knowledge, and close relationship to the Prophet. Though writing as a historian rather than a partisan, al-Tabari's work reflects the respect Imam Ali commanded across the early Muslim world.

Jalal al-Din Rumi (Persian Sufi poet)

Rumi frequently referred to Imam Ali in his poetry as a symbol of spiritual chivalry and inner strength. He saw him as a man who combined outward courage with inward purity.

For Rumi, Imam Ali represented the human being who fights injustice in the world while also conquering the ego within.

Saadi of Shiraz (Persian poet)

Saadi praised Imam Ali as a model of justice and generosity. In his ethical writings, he presented Imam Ali as an example of moral excellence, someone whose actions reflected the highest standards of character.

Allama Muhammad Iqbal (South Asian philosopher and poet)

Iqbal referred to Imam Ali as a figure who united action with spiritual insight. In his poetry, he described Imam Ali as a man whose courage came from faith and whose strength was shaped by his closeness to the Prophet. For Iqbal, Imam Ali represented the ideal fusion of intellect, spirituality, and moral bravery.

Across these voices, something consistent appears. These individuals came from different centuries, languages, and beliefs. Some were Christians. Some were Hindus. Some were Sunnis. Some were Shias. Some were secular historians. Some were poets and philosophers. But when they encountered Imam Ali, they saw similar qualities.

They saw a man of justice who did not bend truth for convenience. They saw a leader who lived humbly even when he ruled. A warrior who preferred mercy over cruelty. A thinker whose words carried moral depth. A human being whose conscience guided every step.

This convergence of voices is not accidental. It reflects the nature of the life they observed. A life lived with sincerity tends to cross boundaries. It does not remain confined to one group or one generation. It travels quietly into the hearts of others.

Imam Ali's memory was not carried only by those who loved him. It was preserved by those who studied him. It was respected by those who analyzed him. It was admired by those who stood outside his tradition.

And when voices from many directions arrive at similar conclusions, their testimony becomes stronger than praise from any single group. It becomes a record of character recognized by humanity itself.

Before We Depart

I stand with a profound sense of gratitude, for the man whose life inspires millions. Now I understand and proudly share that Imam Ali is not a chapter in history; he is a living legend, a living example, a standard, a reminder of what the human being is capable of when guided by truth, humility, and compassion.

Writing about Imam Ali, peace be upon him has not been a task of scholarship alone. It has been a journey of reflection. With each chapter, I discovered something about him, and something about myself. And I hope that as you read, you discover something about yourself too. His story is meant to reach you, stir you, awaken you, and stay with you long after you place this book back on your shelf.

His footsteps do not fade with time. They echo in every heart that seeks dignity, fairness, honesty, courage, and inner strength. They remind us that leadership without ethics is hollow, that knowledge without humility is dangerous, and that power without compassion is destructive. If the noble life of Imam Ali as humbly presented in this book touched you, let that feeling move forward into your life. Let his example be your guide. Let his wisdom reflect in your behavior and action. Let his compassion continue and lived.

If you ever doubt your ability to rise, to forgive, to endure, to lead, or to love, remember him. Remember the man who walked through hardship with grace, who carried truth with courage, and who embraced humanity with tenderness.

May his life strengthen yours. May his character become your compass. May his light guide your steps in moments when the world dims around you.

Thank you for walking through his story with me. May you carry his human spirit wherever you go.

And remember:

"People are either your brother in faith or your equal in humanity."

Imam Ali

My Final Reflection

I find myself reflecting not necessarily only on the life of Imam Ali, but on the private transformation that takes place when one studies a man of such moral clarity. Writing about him is not an academic exercise. It is a journey inward. It is an invitation to examine one's own choices, one's own heart, one's own intentions. For me, this journey of introducing Imam Ali to you my readers, began as an attempt to honor a towering figure in history. It ends as a personal testimony to the power of a noble soul.

Imam Ali's life does not simply inform the mind; it humbles the heart. It reminds us that greatness is not measured by victories or titles, but by the consistency of one's character, the sincerity of one's actions, and the purity of one's conscience. When I walked through his story, his courage, his wisdom, his humility, his struggles, his patience, his justice, and his compassion, I realized that the world has known many leaders, but very few human beings who lived their values so completely.

Iman Ali taught through his silence as much as through his words. He led by example long before leadership theories were written. He fought battles not for ego but for principle. He forgave not to appear virtuous but because his heart could not hold hatred. He embraced poverty when it protected dignity. He turned away from power when it threatened unity. He remained truthful and compassionate when compassion cost him alliances. Such a life cannot be studied without leaving an imprint on one's own.

In Imam Ali, I found a definition of leadership the world desperately needs: leadership grounded in ethics, elevated by humility, sustained by courage, and softened by compassion. Leadership that begins with the heart before it reaches the hand. Leadership that sees humanity before it sees position. Leadership that stays nestled in principle even when the world pulls in every direction.

But above all, Imam Ali reminded me, and I hope reminded you, that the highest form of greatness is goodness. That a noble heart outlives kingdoms. That a sincere soul outshines power. That the footprints of a just man remain long after the dust of time covers everything else.

As a narrator of authentic history, I have spent my life studying individuals, leaders, people, cultures, systems, and the nature of power. In Imam Ali, I found what every seeker, every leader, every parent, every believer, and every human being hopes to find: a map to a meaningful life. A life not free of hardship but full of purpose. A life not untouched by pain but undefeated by it. A life that shows what it means to remain human in moments that tempt us to become anything but.

If this book has moved you, it is because his story carries a depth few lives ever reach. If it has inspired you, it is because his example awakens in each of us the desire to be better, kinder, more courageous, and more compassionate.

References

Recommended Readings

Al-Majlisi, M. B. (1983). *Bihar al-Anwar* (Vols. 1–110). Beirut: Dar Ihya' al-Turath al-'Arabi.

Al-Murtada, A. (1994). *Al-Shafi fi al-Imamah.* Qum: Mu'assasat al-Nashr al-Islami.

Al-Radi, A. (Trans.). (1984). *Nahj al-Balagha: Peak of Eloquence* (M. A. Fadlallah, Trans.). Beirut: Dar al-Ta'aruf.

Al-Tabari, M. J. (1987–1999). *The History of al-Tabari* (Vols. 1–40). Albany, NY: State University of New York Press.

Al-Tusi, S. (1970). *Al-Amali.* Najaf: Al-Maktaba al-Haydariyya.

Al-Ya'qubi, A. (1960). *Tarikh al-Ya'qubi.* Najaf: Al-Matba'ah al-Haydariyya.

Ayoub, M. M. (1988). *Redemptive suffering in Islam: A study of the devotional aspects of Ashura in Twelver Shi'ism.* The Hague: Mouton.

Dakake, M. M. (2011). *The charismatic community: Shi'ite identity in early Islam.* Albany, NY: State University of New York Press.

Donner, F. M. (2010). *Muhammad and the believers: At the origins of Islam.* Cambridge, MA: Harvard University Press.

Hodgson, M. G. S. (1974). *The venture of Islam: Conscience and history in a world civilization* (Vols. 1–3). Chicago, IL: University of Chicago Press.

Husain, S. A. (1996). *The political thought of Imam Ali.* Qum: Ansariyan Publications.

Ibn Abi al-Hadid, A. H. (1964). *Sharh Nahj al-Balagha* (Vols. 1–20). Cairo: Dar Ihya' al-Kutub al-'Arabiyya.

Jafri, S. H. M. (1979). *The origins and early development of Shi'a Islam.* London: Longman.

Madelung, W. (1997). *The succession to Muhammad: A study of the early caliphate.* Cambridge: Cambridge University Press.

Momen, M. (1985). *An introduction to Shi'i Islam: The history and doctrines of Twelver Shi'ism.* New Haven, CT: Yale University Press.

Modarressi, H. (1993). *Crisis and consolidation in the formative period of Shi'ite Islam.* Princeton, NJ: Darwin Press.

Tabataba'i, M. H. (1975). *Shi'ite Islam.* Albany, NY: State University of New York Press.

About Dr. Abraham Khoureis, Ph.D.

Dr. Abraham Khoureis, Ph.D., is a multi-talented thought leader and partner, a global thinker, author, narrator of authentic history, an award-winning mentor, and advocate for compassionate leadership. He is an adjunct professor who specializes in teaching graduate-level courses in business and management, blending academic theory with real-world business practices. Dr. Khoureis is also a small business owner and holds numerous state certifications and professional designations and licenses, highlighting his multidisciplinary expertise.

He is the creator of the Compassionate Leadership Model and Pyramid, which emphasizes leadership built on self-awareness, mindfulness, and commitment to serving others without expectation of return. This seven-level model pyramid, with "Community" as its 5th level, reflects his vision of leadership that positively impacts the broader community and society.

Moreover, Dr. Khoureis developed the Disability Learning Attainment Model, a framework designed to empower individuals with disabilities through inclusive education, skill-building, and leadership development. His work champions and empowers inclusivity, accessibility, and ethical practices in both education and leadership. He has been published on *Forbes.com, Newsweek.com*, and the distinguished *Leader to Leader Journal*. He was recognized as

LinkedIn's Top Leadership and Management Voice, and Thinkers360's Top 50 Voices.

Dr. Abraham's contributions extend to his writings, professional development initiatives, and thought leadership, making him a respected emerging leader in the fields of compassionate leadership, organizational behavior, and human resources development.

Other Books by Dr. Abraham Khoureis, Ph.D.

To access Dr. Abraham latest published books, readily accessible at:

DrAbeKhoureis.com - DrAbeBooks.com

Social Media: DrAbeKhoureis

On Amazon.com, search for Dr. Abraham Khoureis

www.ingramcontent.com/pod-product-compliance
Lightning Source LLC
LaVergne TN
LVHW020715110826
845149LV00012B/2276